S0-CFA-080

THE
DEEPER
THE ROOTS

THE DEEPER THE ROOTS

A MEMOIR OF HOPE AND HOME

MICHAEL TUBBS

FLATIRON
BOOKS
NEW YORK

Note: Some names are changed to protect the privacy of those involved.

THE DEEPER THE ROOTS. Copyright © 2021 by Michael Tubbs.
All rights reserved. Printed in the United States of America. For information,
address Flatiron Books, 120 Broadway, New York, NY 10271.

www.flatironbooks.com

Grateful acknowledgment is made for permission to reproduce from the following:

"The Rose That Grew from Concrete" by Tupac Shakur

All photographs courtesy of the author unless otherwise noted

Designed by Jonathan Bennett

Library of Congress Cataloging-in-Publication Data

Names: Tubbs, Michael, 1990– author.
Title: The deeper the roots : a memoir of hope and home / Michael Tubbs.
Description: First edition. | New York, NY : Flatiron Books, 2021.
Identifiers: LCCN 2021021941 | ISBN 9781250173447 (hardcover) |
    ISBN 9781250173454 (ebook)
Subjects: LCSH: Tubbs, Michael, 1990– | Stanford University—Alumni and
    alumnae—Biography. | African American mayors—California—Stockton—
    Biography. | African American politicians—California—Stockton—Biography. |
    Stockton (Calif.)—Politics and government—21st century. | Stockton (Calif.)—
    Biography.
Classification: LCC F869.S8 T83 2021 | DDC 979.4/054092 [B]—dc23
LC record available at https://lccn.loc.gov/2021021941

Our books may be purchased in bulk for promotional, educational,
or business use. Please contact your local bookseller or the Macmillan Corporate
and Premium Sales Department at 1-800-221-7945, extension 5442, or
by email at MacmillanSpecialMarkets@macmillan.com.

First Edition: 2021

10 9 8 7 6 5 4 3 2 1

For Malakai and Nehemiah: You deserve a world where roses grow on rosebushes.

CONTENTS

Introduction   1

1. She-daddy's Son   5

2. All Eyes on Me   23

3. School Daze   35

4. Dreams   51

5. Hustle and Motivate   71

6. Boy Meets World   85

7. Can I Live?   103

8. Rejection and Redirection   115

9. Sprint   127

10. Victory Lap   147

11. Roses from Concrete   161

12. Upset the Setup   177

13. Keys to the City   191

14. Jericho Road   215

Epilogue: God's Plan   245

Acknowledgments   255

This is a true story, though some names
have been changed.

THE
DEEPER
THE ROOTS

INTRODUCTION

Don't tell nobody our business." This was the mantra my She-daddy (mom) drilled into me before I even started school. I never interrogated it—we didn't have anything to hide, and it's not like I had anything noteworthy to share. Our circumstances were my normal. Things that were tough about our lives were reasons, she said, to prove *Them* wrong.

Them were ubiquitous and circumstantial. At times *Them* were my teachers, at times *Them* was society at large, at times—as far as young me was concerned—*Them* was She-daddy herself. Our business, and by extension my story, never occurred to me as a reason that I wouldn't do well. She-daddy just stressed that I would have to work twice as hard to succeed. Our business became my secret source of strength. Whatever milestone I passed, only my family knew the full distance I'd traveled to the finish line.

By the start of my senior year of high school, as a seventeen-year-old, I had found another reason to keep things to myself. I didn't want to be *just* my story, our business, my origins. (Still don't.) I didn't want to be a statistic. Truthfully, I was ashamed of some parts, of how it all started for us. The poverty, the single parenthood, the struggle all sounded like a stereotypical sob story, and I resolved not to tell it.

Only thing was—I wanted an A in drama class. That summer I had immersed myself in books about the college admissions process, dreaming about hazy green lawns far from Stockton. Every book and article stressed the same thing: that grades and test scores weren't enough, you had to give them a sense of who you *were*. My drama teacher, Mr. Motroni, offered extra credit that fall: enter an essay contest hosted by Alice Walker, responding to the prompt "How I changed my own life." Here was an opportunity to knock out two birds with one stone: get my grade up, and practice for my college admissions essay. I could tell just a little bit of my story, maybe.

As I started writing, I felt as though I was taking a huge inhale and exhale. Finally, I had an outlet to record the experience of my mom's omnipresence and my dad's absence. I smiled as my pen described my mom's strength and determination, how she had given birth when she was my age and had never left me since. I didn't want to embarrass her, but I decided to include this stuff anyway. It was because she only had a high school education, after all, that I was writing this essay, that I was trying to gain acceptance to the best schools in the country.

I struggled with whether to actually mention my father. Nobody outside of my immediate family knew why he wasn't around. My explanation changed each time I was asked—I didn't know who he was, or he moved out of state, or he was dead. All of these were lies. In the end, I opened my essay with the truth: "The first time I saw my father, he was chained." My father was in prison and wasn't getting out anytime soon.

The ink flowed. I wrote about growing up in Stockton, I wrote about the lessons I had learned from my parents. I wrote about how my dreams were incubated in their disappointments and nightmares. I wrote about the context of racism and classism I was just beginning to understand, without which neither my mother's perseverance nor my father's shame made sense to me, and against the tides of which I had accomplished everything I had so early in my life. I wrote about fighting against the soft bigotry of low expectations. It would take me years more to process it all (and I'm still processing!), but I had the first inklings then that my "business" was part of something much bigger. That my "business" was a source of strength and was worthy to be spoken of.

More than a decade later, I understand that stories are important because, *They overcame by the blood of the Lamb and the word of their testimony.* Our testimonies are sources of pride and reservoirs of strength. Storytelling—truth-telling—is how we make sense of the world as it is and gain the vision and courage to create the world as it should be.

In that vein, I see my calling not as a political one, but as a narrative one. I am more a griot than a politician and, to quote my favorite rapper, J. Cole: "My story ain't the only story I'm trying to tell." The aim of this book and of my work is to share what deserves to be shouted from the rooftops. Trauma and triumph. Pain and purpose. A story of Stockton and cities like it. Of policy failures. Of growing up Black and poor in post-Reagan America. Of being the path-breaking mayor of a major American city during the Trump presidency. Of mass incarceration. The story of my mom, my aunt, and grandmother, and countless single mothers like them. The story of my father. A story of progress and of pitfalls. A story of making history. My story.

I won that essay contest, by and by. In one of the many lucky, surreal turns my life has taken, I got to meet Ms. Alice Walker, who gave me some words I'll never forget. She helped me realize that my life is not a sob story, but a survivor's tale.

Thank you, Alice Walker. And thank *you*, for reading on.

1

SHE-DADDY'S SON

He was despised and rejected by mankind,
a man of suffering, familiar with pain.

My voice faltered. I looked down, tried to power through it, but I suddenly felt too overwhelmed to finish the passage. I stood before hundreds of congregants on the biggest Sunday of the year, Easter, my face wet with tears. I was eleven, and I wasn't crying because I was nervous, or because I had messed up. I was crying because it, the story of Jesus, was messed up. When I had practiced this passage with my mom, I'd kept my emotions in check. I saved my tears for when I missed a word, which carried the threat of a quick lash of the belt.

Before the congregation, however, the tears flowed freely. The injustice, the grief—the loneliness of it all.

Yet it was our pain that he bore,
our sufferings he endured.

In Sunday School, four years prior, we were given short verses to memorize for the Christmas program from Luke, chapter 2. Sister Kim gave me Luke 2:1–3, but when I had committed that to memory I decided to read more. The next Sunday during class, I eagerly raised my hand and told Sister Kim that I had memorized not just my verse, but verses 1–14.

To humor me or to call my bluff, she asked me to recite it on the spot, which I did. "And it came to pass in those days that a decree went out from Caesar Augustus . . ." The account of Jesus' birth. After church, Sister Kim told Pastor Alfred what I'd done, and he had me recite it for the Christmas program in front of the entire congregation. I was seven years old and terrified of all the people looking at me, but the words just flowed. I received a standing ovation. Pastor Alfred took up an offering, and gave me the money.

After that, it became a thing. Pastor Alfred asking me to memorize chapters of the Bible to share with the congregation. Every Christmas, every Easter, every church special occasion, every time a young person was needed to spice up the program—I was called upon. Every time I asked him if I had to, he would reply, "Yes."

"I see something in you," he would continue. "God has plans for your life."

Pastor Alfred was a dreamer. He had graduated from Franklin High School in Stockton and, with not much more than a dream, sold his car for six hundred dollars to make the first rent payment on the humble downtown building his church originally occupied. Before long the congregation had outgrown that space and moved into a real church building, an A-frame with colorful stained glass that ran from the floor to the roofline at the front of the church. Booming into the mic, he sounded as much like a motivational speaker as a minister, reminding us that God wanted us to pursue greatness. He made me the chair of the Youth Leadership Team. He made me feel like I mattered.

But that Easter Sunday, I felt like I'd blown it.

Pastor Smith came and gave me a hug as I finished, and I saw Nana beaming with pride. But Mom looked horrified. She grabbed me and whisked me out of church before anyone could talk to us.

As we got in the car, her face was grim. She was strict with me—she could, at times, give Joe Jackson a run for his money. I had to turn out *perfect*. It was her life's work. And here I was messing up my unlikely chance at the pulpit. Not to mention that her own experience in front of a congregation had been one of the most humiliating of her life.

To fully understand my mom's reaction, you need to know a little more about her, and about the place where this all happened: my hometown of Stockton, California.

For generations, Stockton was seen as a place to run toward, not away from. Its original inhabitants, the Miwok and the Yokut, knew this: their hunter and gatherer societies thrived in a valley that teemed with elk, deer, antelopes, bears, beavers and rabbits, ducks and geese, blackberries, acorns and pine nuts, and vast stocks of fish. The Spanish colonizers, arriving from Mexico in the late 1700s to establish their missions, knew it too, as did the French-Canadian fur trappers who traveled down from Vancouver and set up the 1828 settlement called French Camp, where they hunted and fished so greedily that within less than two decades they'd depleted the animal populations and had to leave again.

Not long after that, the promise and opportunity of the area became apparent to the rest of the world. Within a year of the discovery of gold in 1848, a hundred thousand people—the infamous forty-niners—had arrived seeking their fortune, most from the East Coast, Latin America, and Europe, but some from as far away as Australia and China too. A Black Freedman from Virginia named William Robison was among them: he worked as a driver transporting gold dust for Wells Fargo and would later become an advocate for civil rights and school desegregation until his death in 1899.

Stockton was perfectly positioned, nestled between the major Pacific seaport and the Mother Lode in the foothills of the Sierra Nevada mountains. The town did a booming business outfitting, provisioning, and entertaining the gold prospectors. In 1850 its population was about one thousand; four years later it was seven times that, making it the fourth-largest city in the state, behind San Francisco, Sacramento, and Marysville.

Once the gold mines were deserted, attention turned from the mountains back to the fertile valley below. New residents not only farmed fields of grain and then other crops, but also opened large flour mills, canned fruits and vegetables, and manufactured farming equipment. The city's elites built themselves grand mansions and impressive churches, a few of which have survived to this day. When the 1906 earthquake devastated San Francisco, many of those fleeing the city came to Stockton, including several thousand Chinese Americans, who would build what became the third-largest Chinatown on the West Coast.

The expansion of agriculture and related industries attracted a steady flow of immigrants. Italians, mostly from the area around Genoa, came and established a macaroni factory and the Genova bakery. Japanese farmers like George "Potato King" Shima were masters in making productive farmland from the delta's swamps. Sikhs from the Punjab region of India came to labor in the fields and built the first Sikh temple in North America in Stockton. During the Great Depression, white farmers from the South and the Midwest arrived by the thousands, until the east side of Stockton came to be known as "Okieville." Thousands of Filipinos arrived in the 1920s and 1930s, creating a thriving Little Manila neighborhood and becoming what would be the largest community of Filipinos outside the Philippines.

In the 1940s, wartime shipbuilding blossomed, employing some ten thousand workers in ten shipyards along the Stockton Channel. Alongside several military bases, this industry drew a lot of African Americans, particularly from the South. Also in the 1940s, the fields producing food for the armed forces needed more laborers, and the government adopted the "bracero" guest worker program to recruit farmworkers from Mexico. One of the program's major proponents was Tillie Lewis, Stockton's groundbreaking female industrialist, the child of Jewish immigrants from the Ukraine, who employed more people than the shipyards in her Flotill canneries. Until her death in 1977, she was known for her open and fair hiring policies that gave many Mexicans and women the ability to attain some independence and wealth. Finally, following the Vietnam War, thousands of refugees from Vietnam, Laos, and Cambodia made their way to Stockton in search of a fresh start.

All told, for some three hundred years, people from all parts of the world were drawn to Stockton by the promise of opportunity. The vestiges remain today: Stockton is the most diverse city in the United States, and the resilience and entrepreneurial spirit of its past is still alive.

Like me, both my parents were raised in Stockton. My mom was born there. My dad's parents moved to Stockton from Jackson, Mississippi, when he was two years old. My grandparents on both sides came to Stockton from other places because they viewed it as a place of promise, of opportunity and fresh starts. My paternal grandparents, John and Ruthie Tubbs, came so that John could become one of the first Black firefighters in the Stockton fire department. My maternal grandfather, Jimmy Dixon, came as a child with his family, heading west in search of work from Texarkana, Arkansas. My nana, Barbara Nicholson, met my papa and joined him in Stockton in the early twenties, thinking there was more opportunity for her in Stockton than in Bakersfield. My grandparents, like those before them, viewed Stockton as a hopeful destination.

As my parents became teenagers, however, the dynamic began to change. The lure of Stockton was becoming the cash to be made in the crack cocaine trade. By the late 1980s, crack in Stockton could net a dealer 400 percent more than they could make in LA, because demand far outpaced supply. Transnational gangs took root, and a reputation for violence and crime began to subsume the city's identity. This transformation was accelerated by the racist policy decisions that made poverty endemic. Because of decades of redlining—the policies that deemed neighborhoods with a majority of Black and Brown residents as too risky to invest in, which resulted in 98 percent of home loans going only to white families between 1934 and 1962—downtown and South Stockton had less and less to offer in the way of amenities and services.

When the city's wealthier and whiter residents moved into the suburbs, those services, everything from banks to grocery stores to better schools, followed them. Stockton became a place that people tried to escape from, looking elsewhere in the state and in the nation for opportunity.

In the early 1960s highways were built to service the suburbs, for which nearly all the grand historic buildings and the vibrant diverse neighborhoods of downtown were demolished, including Little Manila, Chinatown, Japantown, and the Mexican El Barrio del Chivo. In a brutal irony, though Stockton was in the midst of the fertile Central Valley, which produced half the fruits and vegetables grown in the United States, there were few supermarkets in the southern part of the city. Many neighborhoods in Stockton became and continue to be food deserts, where the only places to buy food or produce are fast-food restaurants or liquor stores.

Despite the changes around them, my aunt and mom grew up much like every other Generation Xer. My nana and papa were divorced, but the sisters spent time with each parent, and had lower-middle-class financial stability given Nana's job with the county government and Papa's military benefits and job with the butcher's union. Papa struggled with PTSD from serving in the conflict in Vietnam and from alcoholism, but my mom and aunt were able to have a fairly standard childhood. Their concerns weren't about safety, or about the land use decisions that created the communities they frequented. They focused on how to navigate the city bus system and what new adventures it could provide them. Leisure time was spent with lifelong friends, walking to the swimming pool, window shopping at the mall, attending drive-in theatres, and going to the local hip skating rink, Hammer Skate.

That all changed in January of 1990, when Racole Dixon stood in front of her family's church, mic in hand, palms sweaty. Her mother, Barbara Nicholson, sat teeth-clenched and stoic in the pews. Pastor Amos introduced Racole with the words of James 5:16, "Therefore confess your sins to each other and pray for each other so that you may be healed."

Sixteen-year-old Racole was suddenly alone at the pulpit. She spoke slowly, robotically, not quite masking the hint of defiance in her voice. "I want to apologize to the congregation and ask for forgiveness. I've already asked God. I am three months' pregnant. I'm stepping down from my post in the youth choir and children's church." Her confession was met with silence, some murmurs, and then a corporate prayer from the congregants. She returned to her seat, where her mother—my nana—gave her a hug and kiss on the cheek.

She rushed to the car immediately after the service and waited for her mom and sister, Tasha, to go home. She didn't cry, she wouldn't let them see her cry, but she was awash with fear and anger. Why did everyone have to know her business? Why weren't everyone's sins showcased this way?

There were no announcement postcards sent. A pregnancy such as this, unplanned and very early, wasn't exactly something to be proud of. Many in the audience she had spoken to, and maybe some in the car, felt that as my life was beginning, hers had just ended.

My dad also had a normal childhood, although he decided to rebel against lower-middle-class conventionality. He was barely a teenager when the action on the streets pulled his attention away from basketball, football, and high school. The Crips had come up from Los Angeles and taken over Stockton; he became a Blood, for no real reason other than they were the underdogs in the turf wars. He didn't like bullies, and fancied himself as everyone's protector and advocate. I guess maybe that's something he passed along to me.

My dad had four brothers and sisters. Despite his father being one of the first Black firefighters in the City of Stockton, he got it into his head that he could make a lot of money selling drugs, and thus shield his siblings from having to get involved in the trade themselves. One day while he was out running the streets, his little brother Calvin borrowed one of his red coats and wore it out. Calvin got jumped because he looked like a Blood. When my dad got home, his mom was out in the backyard, stoking a bonfire into which she was throwing all his red clothes.

"You ain't gonna be bringing this kind of stuff into the house!" she yelled.

The fire mirrored his passion for the street life. He left the house and developed a "new family" while hanging around a place called Gleason Park, then the center of the Stockton drug trade. Dubbed "a million-dollar spot," Gleason had earned its reputation as a place where thugs and addicts freely shot up, and crime was rampant despite being just a few blocks from the police department and city hall. There, people gravitated toward my father. Some of his friends called him "The Mayor."

At thirteen, he got a gun. All he'd had to do was tell someone he needed one. His fire and passion for what he perceived as being "the underdog" continued to burn, and he gained a reputation for fighting anybody, and a nickname—G-Whack, like wacky, crazy.

His real name is Michael Tubbs.

Hammer Skate, a roller-skating rink on Hammer Lane on the north side of Stockton, had been the place to be on the weekends since the late seventies. Over the years the soundtrack changed from Donna Summer and "Funky Town" remixes to "Thriller" and De La Soul, while the fashion went from bellbottoms and fringed suede to spandex and satin jackets. The vibe was always good. There was a dark corner where the teens could make out, unseen, while their parents chitchatted at the other end of the rink. A lot of first kisses happened there.

My dad's cousin rolled on up to him one night and said, "My girl Koco wanna talk to you."

His cousin was best friends with a sixteen-year-old girl named Koco: Racole Dixon. Mom. She was known as a good church girl, which belied her rebellious streak. Her mom, Barbara, was super strict, but she had an irresistible attraction to bad boys. She and seventeen-year-old Dad struck up a conversation, exchanged numbers, and even couple-skated.

They started hooking up on the regular—even though he had to travel into Crip territory, enemy territory, to visit her. Only a few months in, she started feeling sick and when she missed her period she got nervous. Without telling anyone, she took the bus across town to Kaiser to take a pregnancy test. When the result came back, her heart dropped. She was a junior in high school; she had always thought kids would happen after she graduated and became an adult.

She considered her options. She had decided not to take birth control, despite being sexually active, so that no one would know she was, in fact, having sex. The thought of abortion flashed through her mind—her secret would remain that, and she could continue to live her life as planned. Otherwise she would have to tell her mother and might be kicked out of her home. She would have to endure the judgments and commentary of people in her church and her school. She would have to take on the responsibility of raising the child herself, she knew, as my dad was constantly on the run from rival gangs or the law and they weren't boyfriend and girlfriend in the traditional sense.

Staring at all those realities, she resolved that even if it was her and the life inside her against the world, she would try. She would go through with the pregnancy and rebel against the easier routes others might have chosen.

The first person she told was her big sister. "Tasha, you want to get something to eat? Let's go to Denny's," was the invitation. Over two Grand Slams, she deputized Tasha with her secret.

"What?! I didn't know you was having sex!" Tasha said, despite that she had picked Mom up from her rendezvous more than once.

"You gotta tell Momma."

The conversation with Momma—Barbara—happened the next day in the living room. "Mom, you know how I haven't been feeling well lately?" my mom stammered, looking at the ground. "Yeah, you're sick. Get some rest." "No, Mom. I'm pregnant," she said, raising her gaze to see Nana's reaction.

Barbara took a deep breath. Multiple emotions warred on her face, but betrayal won out. "How could you?! You know better! You go to Catholic school. You was raised in the Church! You know the Word." The seriousness of the hurt was belied by her resolve, though. She locked eyes with Racole and said: "You're not gonna get no abortion. You don't know who you're carrying inside you." They both cried, relieved. Racole had already decided to go through with the pregnancy.

Nana called my dad and his mother over to her house. She started the meeting with questions that would normally be asked at the onset of a courtship. "What are you planning to do with your life?" My father mumbled that he didn't even know, that he hadn't even finished high school yet. Nana cut him off: "We'll figure it out. We're gonna get together and we're gonna raise a good child."

Complications came quickly for my father. In June 1990, he graduated high school. In July, he wound up in the California Youth Authority (CYA)[1], a prison for youth offenders. He and his friend who was a fellow Blood had gone into Crips territory and the friend left my dad there by himself. Disloyalty. Betrayal. A major strike. To get back at him, my dad shot his former friend in the leg the next time he saw him. Everybody survived. Street justice was satisfied. But the police found out and he got locked up for three years.

The California Youth Authority is widely considered a training ground for prison, filled with chaos and violence, and the deferred aspirations of young men caught in a vicious system. While my mom dealt with morning sickness, my dad was developing a sickness of his own: CYA introduced him to heroin.

On August 2, 1990, Racole, Barbara, and Tasha were watching the *Oprah Winfrey Show* when my nana, Barbara, realized

---

1 CYA was renamed the Division of Juvenile Justice in 2005 in an effort to rebrand itself after CYA became synonymous with cruelty, abuse, and deaths of inmates.

her daughter's pants were soaking wet. Racole's water had broken, and in a panic they rushed to the hospital.

The doctor was not reassuring. I was a month early, and he said the labor needed to be held off because my lungs weren't fully enough developed for me to survive. "You can't have him yet," was his final prognosis. The hospital arranged for a chopper to be ready to take me to a hospital in Oakland in case I came out too soon anyway. After a frantic call from Nana, Pastor Amos and Pastor Taylor came to her room at the hospital and prayed.

As Racole's contractions intensified, the hospital staff still didn't believe she was in labor. As is often the case with Black women, particularly those who are poor and young, they heard her cries as exaggerations, her feelings as ignorance. They had made a mistake hooking up the monitor that tracked her contractions; the pain she shared with them wasn't made up, it didn't register on their monitor because of their incompetence. In desperation, Racole rushed into the shower to alleviate the excruciating pain with hot water on her back. Suddenly my head was crowning.

They got the helicopter ready.

But I came out with my lungs fully developed, though I had a heart murmur and was still a premature baby. My mom held me close as I took my first breaths. She looked at Nana and said, "The devil was trying to take him before he was born."

Nana was beside herself with joy. As she held me, all anger and disappointment at my mom's pregnancy dissipated. She announced that I would call her Nana because she was too young at forty-two to be a grandmother. Auntie Tasha was proud of her sister's courage. All three, despite not having a formal conversation, resolved in that hospital to serve as a band of three mothers, committing to raise me right by any means necessary.

My dad found out about my birth from his counselor in the prison, who called him into her office to deliver the news. When he went back to his cell, he broke down and wailed. The first tears he'd shed since his incarceration—bitter tears. My mom and I visited him when I was two weeks old. He held me in his arms our whole visit, and was proud that I didn't cry at all.

No one believed that my mother was going to graduate high school with a baby. Not on time, with her class, anyway. Nana was so certain of this fact that she made my mom a promise: she would get her a car if she graduated on time. But if her own mother had given up dreams for her future, my mom was determined to prove her, and everyone else, wrong. She worked hard, and with support from my aunt, managed to balance books and papers, with bottles and Pampers. I was her escort to school during her senior year, where she dropped me off at the on-site daycare because Nana had a full-time job and was not going to give that up to serve as my full-time nanny. When I was two years old, Racole graduated high school right on schedule.

At graduation, she walked up the steps to the stage alone, but as soon as she was handed her diploma, she reached out to Tasha, who ran on the floor with me in tow, and took me in her arms too. An infant in one arm and her high school diploma in the other. As she smiled for pictures, her grin revealed her satisfaction at accomplishing a difficult feat that many had told her, in words or with pitying eyes, would be impossible for her to accomplish.

She was also probably excited to get her car keys.

That same year, at age nineteen, Michael was released from

CYA. Nana and my mom allowed him to take me to his mom's house every weekend. He had no clue what he was doing with a baby, but he did well enough, all while trying to kick his heroin habit. He'd go get clean for a while, and then start up again, but managed to hide it throughout. On the surface everything was under control, while within he fought his demons.

Nana was committed to raising me, but the détente with her teenage daughter didn't last past my toddlerhood. She kicked my mom out of the house at nineteen for "acting crazy," when her daughter's retorts to any question about her whereabouts, her plans—anything—became unbearable. Nana said I could stay, and tried to give me a kiss and a hug to let me know that she wasn't upset with me, but Mom wasn't having any of it. She packed all of our clothes in two trash bags and left in the car she had won in the graduation bet.

Kicked out of Nana's house, we were homeless. Mom sought refuge in a shelter, but found the congregate living setting extremely uncomfortable. She worked with Tasha to access vouchers that allowed us shelter in motel rooms. These vouchers meant intrusive paperwork and pleading with case managers, but ultimately they prevailed. We stayed in a Motel 6 for about a month, while my mom worked and saved for the three months' rent required for a place of our own. She would sit me on her lap by the pool after a long day's work, telling me we were on a vacation. During those one-sided conversations she whispered affirmations about how one day I would have a pool in my backyard, or that I would take my family on vacations to nicer hotels than this one.

Mom finally found a place in downtown Stockton, on Oak Street. In its heyday downtown Stockton had bustled with activity, the center of the civic life and home to thriving ethnic communities and businesses. We arrived to an area made lifeless through redlining and disinvestment, joining a community with the shortest life expectancy in the city, and the highest rates of asthma, crime, diabetes, and infant mortality. But it wasn't a shelter. It wasn't Motel 6. It was the best my mother could do at the time, and it was home for six years.

It wasn't home because of a fully stocked fridge—the only thing in there most days was government cheese, huge, ungrated blocks of cheese that we received as part of the WIC and welfare programs. If we weren't eating over at Tasha's or at Nana's (after they reconciled), Mom got creative with staples like fried bologna, alpine hotdogs, and Spam. It wasn't home because of welcoming neighbors; Mom made it a point for us not to talk to anyone as we came home at night, and to lock the doors when we entered. Lullabies and bedtime stories were complete with neighborhood gunshots in the background. It wasn't home because of the neighborhood markets, although I relished our trips to the local liquor store on weekends, using food stamps to buy quarter jerky and sour punch ropes. No: it was home because despite the hardship, Mom always made sure that the lights were on and that I never felt alone. Aware of the odds stacked against me, even from that young age, she would make sure that my vision was vertical instead of horizontal. In ways big and small, she stressed that the struggles we faced weren't permanent, weren't indicative of my worth, and weren't my fault.

My dad, meanwhile, was arrested again, on a drug violation. On Valentine's Day, 1996, he pulled up on some guys that he knew were in the drug game, and forced them into a car at gunpoint. He drove them to where they held their money and stole thirty-seven hundred dollars from them. He figured that because of street code, they wouldn't testify (or "snitch") against him. Even if they were rivals, he was sure they were united in the conviction that the justice system was not the way to address wrongs.

He was wrong.

He didn't realize his error until later that year, when, two weeks after my sixth birthday, he was arrested for a double count of kidnap-robbery. His sentence was harsh. By virtue of California's Three Strikes law, he was given seven years to life plus seven years to life, plus eighteen years bowlegged, meaning he'd have to complete the eighteen years before he started on the seven-to-life sentences.

As a six-year-old, I had no concept of the length of time Michael was sentenced to serve, and didn't attend his trial. I didn't expect consistency in when I saw him as it was. I did, however, have a concept that I would see him eventually— and as his absence stretched on I grew anxious. Mom, Tasha, or Nana never sat me down to explain to me his crime, or for how long he would be away. I became an angry child, because I was mad at my dad. I was mad at the powerlessness to do anything to change that, and the information vacuum that ensued was filled with the provocations of a child trying to figure out why his father was gone, and, more important, why he had to go without a father. In hindsight, they never shared, and I guess I was too afraid to ask, afraid of what the nature of his crime or length of his incarceration would signal or prophesy about me.

A man of suffering, familiar with pain
like one from whom you turn your face.

The women in my family—Mom, Tasha, and Nana: my three mothers—never spoke directly about what Michael's sentence meant for their role in my life. What is understood doesn't have to be explained. They closed ranks to ensure that I would be imprisoned by their love and fierce desire for my story to end differently than Michael Anthony Tubbs'.

> *By oppression and judgment he was taken away.*
> *Yet who of his generation protested?*

The ride back home on Easter Sunday was silent and long. I stared out the window, brooding that I hadn't wanted to recite the Scriptures in the first place, and annoyed at how my mom had a gift for finding fault in anything. She stared straight ahead, her lips pursed. "I didn't cry because I messed up," I had explained as we walked to the car, "I cried because something came over me and I just felt heavy."

Inside the house, my mom's glare turned into a look of bewilderment as our phone greeted us with the red light blinking. The voicemail was overwhelmed with messages from church members. They called to say how moving they found my vulnerability, that they had never really *heard* the passage on Jesus' death before that day. My recitation had opened something up in them, member after member said; my tears had allowed them to be more attuned to the suffering and weight of those words. What my mom believed was a mortifying mistake had turned into a testimony to the grace of the community.

Grace is both necessary and sufficient to power us through hard times, I would learn. Grace and the love of fierce women were the nutrients I needed to grow in the soil I was planted in: Stockton, California.

2

ALL EYES ON ME

What does *your* mom do, Michael?"

It was a question my mom must have seen coming, given her already constant warnings not to tell anyone our "business." I couldn't escape it at Lakeside Christian Elementary School. My four years there would be the first of many times I've straddled the lines of class, race, and other privileges, building the determination to succeed combined with a She-daddy–sized rebellious streak.

Auntie Tasha had found Lakeside, a private academy that educated many of Stockton's middle- and upper-class children, through hours of research and questioning. Both Tasha and my mom had asked their supervisors' supervisors where they sent their children to school. Lakeside cost three hundred dollars per month per child, and we all went—myself and my cousins, Tasha's daughters Shaleeka and Scharlyce—thanks to Papa's military pension, which covered tuition.

Before my very first day, my mom gave me a pep talk. She pulled me close and, with that determined look she often had in her eye, reminded me that I would be going to school with doctors' kids and lawyers' kids. "But you're just as smart," she said. "You'll do fine." She had at least one reason for confidence: I *loved* to read.

It was Auntie Tasha, again, who had nurtured my love of books. She took my cousin Shaleeka and I—only eight months apart—to the library for story time as toddlers, where we sat glued to our spots, always more interested in the stories than running around the library like some of the other kids. As I grew older, every time I went to the library I'd take out ten books at a time, lug them home with me, and come back for another batch a week or two later. Auntie Tasha made sure to incorporate Black history in our early reading, introducing stories of Black achievement and Black excellence. We learned of the Anansi the Spider books of African tales and of *Henry's Freedom Box*, by Ellen Levine. In fourth, fifth, and sixth grade, I wrote my final book report on each one of Frederick Douglass's autobiographies. We were given an idea of what it meant to be Black at an early age, an idea that was rooted in assets and pride, instead of deficits and shame.

Church was also a source of reading material. After I recited my verses for the Christmas program, the next Sunday Sister Kim told me to follow her to her car after the service. She had a bag filled to the brim with books that she bequeathed to me, telling me these were some of the books her children enjoyed, and she would give me new books every month. Sister Kim and her husband were both doctors, and their kids went to MIT and Stanford for college. The books she gave me were classics. Madeleine L'Engle. Roald Dahl. C. S. Lewis. Everything by Charles Dickens. Walter Dean Myers. Lois Lowry. J. R. R. Tolkein. The Hardy Boys. I devoured them all.

My moms (She-daddy and Auntie Tasha) realized that books were a comfort to me, and that I would read anything and everything I could put my hands on. This realization turned into the brilliant idea to create an incentive structure of buying me even more books when I received straight A's, to "keep the A's coming," as Tasha was fond of saying. I would spend hours at Barnes & Noble, claiming my prize and exasperating everyone with my indecision around what to buy. At the laundromat, on the way to basketball practice, in the bathtub, in most of my nonstructured time, I was reading.

Books broadened my horizons and allowed me to conceive of a world different from the one I was living in. A world where the protagonist had ultimate agency, where failure was never the destination and disappointments were rare obstacles, as opposed to the status quo.

Meanwhile, the world in our neighborhood remained mostly off-limits. I spent most of my time at school, at church, and at Tasha's or Nana's (my grandmother's), only coming home to sleep. The only grocery store within a five-mile radius was the liquor store, and the closest bank was a check-cashing place. After stopping there, my mom would reenter the car with anguish on her face, telling me to never, ever use check-cashing services if I wanted to stay out of debt.

In the complex was a communal dumpster. I hated taking out the trash because, as soon as the bag hit the dumpster, several cats would jump out aggressively. Rottweilers and pit bulls patrolled the streets, some with their owners, others without them. I didn't know any of my neighbors that well, and neither did my mom. There was no asking for sugar, or for help, or even routine get-to-know-you questions. Mom was adamant about limiting my contact with this part of the world. Subconsciously, she was trying to tell herself and me to not get too comfortable nor too attached here—that this was not going to be our permanent home. At least I had my books.

My new friends at Lakeside invited me over to their houses, and it was the first time I saw how well-off people lived. Nice big houses. Pools in the backyards. Lots of trees and manicured lawns. A whole other side of Stockton. A whole other world, really. In these castles, in between ducking defenders to score on their basketball court, I was constantly dodging questions from my friends' parents. "What does your mom do, Michael?" The questions were always posed with a faintly accusatory tone.

"I don't know," was my favorite refrain. That answer generally impeded progression to "What does your dad do?" Even when I didn't answer their questions, I learned that some of these parents were ready to share their opinions and judgments with me. At a weeklong science camp, nervous in line for a rock climbing wall, I sang to myself absentmindedly a song Mom and I listened to at home, featuring Snoop Dogg and called "Wrong Idea." "I want the world to see I'm a gangsta," I mumbled. Unexpectedly, a chaperone on the trip went out of her way to make sure that I knew she agreed.

"That's right," she said. "You're nothing but a little gangster."

I knew people like her were trying to see if I actually belonged in their world.

The school dress code didn't help. It called for collared shirts and khakis from Nordstrom, and my mom could only afford four shirts—yet we could only get to the laundromat on weekends. I did my best to keep my shirts clean for reuse during the week, but I am messy and not terribly conscientious. On the occasions when my shirts were too soiled to be worn again, I had to borrow one of Shaleeka's, which, because it was a girl's shirt, had a ruffled collar. When a classmate grabbed my collar and informed the class that "MT is wearing a girl's shirt!" I found myself repeating the laundry story in the principal's office, having unleashed on the kid about his bad grades and ugly shoes.

The discrepancies between what I saw at my house and what I saw at my friends' houses—and sometimes my own weird shirts—made me super competitive in the classroom. I had to be the best, period.

I especially relished when I knew I had done better than classmates whose parents contributed heavily to their work. "Wait, didn't your mom help you with that? How many did you miss? You missed three? Isn't your mom a lawyer? I missed zero," I yelled across class one day as the teacher handed back our graded work.

"Michael," my teacher warned.

"What? I'm just saying." And boom, I was kicked out of class. Again. For being disruptive. For talking back. For being defiant.

I had a love-hate relationship with all of my teachers. Love for those who viewed me as a child to cultivate and challenge, and hate for those who viewed me as something that needed to be controlled. Mrs. Carter, my sixth-grade teacher, got me; she would have me grade other students' work or give me extra work to do. She'd call me up to her desk and challenge me with questions, or with middle-school textbooks to keep me occupied and not making my classmates laugh. Other teachers would say only that I was a "distraction," not noticing that I was bored because I had finished the work and needed something else to do. One teacher threatened to retire because I was in her class.

I loved class, when I was allowed to remain in it. I was quick to raise my hand, to ask questions, to not take things at face value, and willing to correct a teacher if a fact was wrong. I guess that rubbed some of my teachers the wrong way, and I was often sent to the office or forced to sit in the hallway outside. The break from the monotony of class, however, freed me to move at my own pace, and to read ahead and let my mind wander.

My moms explained to me before and after inevitable parent-teacher conferences that some teachers didn't like to be challenged in front of the class, or weren't used to a student like me, and that I would need to be more measured. I didn't listen; I had a growing chip on my shoulder. A paradox was becoming apparent: I was always on the principal's honor roll for having straight A's and also was almost always *in* the principal's office.

I didn't have the language then, but I had a latent suspicion that it had something to do with being one of the few Black students at Lakeside. I noticed how I was constantly kicked out for "defiance" for doing things my classmates were allowed to do without reprimand. I noticed that I saw most of the students who looked like me in the office, rather than onstage with me during the academic awards ceremonies. I noticed how my school community looked different than my church and home community. The only thing in my neighborhood that reminded me of my teachers were the cops that patrolled our streets.

My sense of injustice wasn't always a hundred percent accurate. Near the end of my sixth grade year, I competed in the regional Math Olympics. I knew I was good at math—Auntie Tasha had convinced the principal to allow me to take a higher grade in the subject, along with one other student whose father was a university math professor. So when it was announced that I didn't even place in the contest, I knew there was some conspiracy. I had been cheated. I went to my mom and Auntie Tasha and tearfully pleaded my case. They believed me, and demanded to see the test. They looked, and looked again.

Literally, I just had a lot of wrong answers. I had lost, but in retrospect I won. I had fearless advocates who believed I was worth fighting for, no matter what.

As I approached middle school, my mom and auntie began their research into where I should go after Lakeside. In the break room, my mom overheard her supervisor's supervisor and a colleague talking about "Pre-IB at Hamilton Middle School." My mom, at twenty-seven, had just bought her first house, a small but brand-new, nice three-bedroom on the south side of Stockton, in a working-class community a five-minute walk from Hamilton. We would drive by the house almost weekly as it was being built, monitoring its progress, Mom always recounting with pride how she was going to own her own home before she was thirty, and that we would be the first people to use the bathroom in it. She had heard Hamilton was a bad school, so she was puzzled to hear a person with means considering it. She inquired about the program and came back home with what she had discovered. "Mike, this program is tough. Lots of kids can't hang with it. It's no joke." And then, of course: "I'm thinking of putting you there."

At first, I protested, as I wanted to stay with the tight-knit Lakeside community into junior high. It was made clear that this wasn't an option, as the academics at the junior high weren't rigorous enough. At the same time, my mom kept stressing how difficult the program at Hamilton was until I took the bait. "Just because their kids struggled in the program doesn't mean I will."

Shaleeka didn't come with me. Tasha had found a small, conservative Baptist school for her to attend with our cousin, Donnell, Tasha's godson and best friend's son. So I went off to attend Hamilton Middle School alone.

Hamilton was the ultimate paradox. It was the only school in the entire county that housed the pre–International Baccalaureate program, a rigorous college preparatory curriculum. Students, many affluent and some white, from all across the county were bussed into my neighborhood to take advantage of the program—so much so that the majority of the students in the program were not students like me, for whom Hamilton was the default neighborhood school. Outside of the International Baccalaureate program, however, Hamilton was like a scene from "The Wire." In the hallways, and especially near the gym, you would find preteens engrossed in complex arithmetic—high-stakes gambling, that is, shooting craps for lunch money and playing quarters. During lunch many of the IB students separated themselves from what our teachers called "the general population students," eating in the classroom for fear of a routine fight or occasional full-scale gang riot. At times, it did feel dangerous. Campus security agreed, as they were apt to put the cafeteria on lockdown.

The adjustment was rough. I didn't feel I had much in common with the students in the IB program besides schoolwork, and I didn't fit in yet with the students outside the program. I had never realized just how sheltered I had been. I was out of my depth, and lonely.

"Mom, no one knows me. I hate it here," I said often. Mom's response was always a hug, coupled with tough love. Another lesson she had drilled into me throughout childhood was to "never let them see you cry," whether at the Math Olympics or losing a basketball game. (Or on Easter Sunday.) It was imperative to let people know that all was "good." In the world we lived in, vulnerability was a sign of weakness.

After about a month, I settled in through the language of basketball. Hoops and my knack for trash-talking allowed me to make friends outside of the IB program, so I didn't have to eat lunch in the classroom. My friends made sure everyone knew that "Tubbs is coo." When the bell rang and we had to return to class, inevitably a competitor or teammate would be shocked that I was headed for the IB classes. Very few students in the program were Black males, and even rarer was one fluent in the cultural competencies that signaled belonging in South Stockton—wearing the right shoes, knowing the right songs and slang, having the same points of reference. Every time I heard, "Nigga, we ain't know you was smart," I took it as a huge compliment.

In the classroom, the pattern from Lakeside continued. I clashed with many teachers, was often kicked out of class, and was almost even kicked out of the program for "disrespect"— all the while maintaining stellar grades. During this time, I read *Soledad Brother* and the *Autobiography of Malcolm X*, seeking to make sense of my clashing experiences. Comments like, "You actually did well" or "How did you know that?" reminded me of the faux compliments Malcolm X received from his teachers, even as they ridiculed his desire to become a lawyer.

I also encountered familiar questions from my friends' parents, about how I had heard about the IB program, where I came from, and why I was doing so well academically. I tutored one friend at his house every other weekend, while his dad studied me with a mix of suspicion and intrigue. After the second weekend, I asked my friend whether his father had a problem with me. He didn't know, but would find out. Back at school he pulled me aside during pass period to share that his father wasn't a hater, just confused.

"By what?"

"Oh. He's a prison guard and he has an inmate in there named Michael Tubbs. Crazy, right?" he said, laughing. "I told him there was no way he could be your dad. Like none. Maybe a cousin or something."

"Weird," I said, and shrugged.

Inside I felt a flurry of emotions. Pride. I was tutoring my father's prison guard's son. Sadness. My friend's dad probably knew mine and definitely saw him more than I did. Anger. My dad was in prison.

My default mode at Hamilton was nonchalance, like everything was fine, like everything was a joke and nothing was a big deal. Inside I was smoldering. Although I couldn't yet articulate why I felt disrespected or unsafe in the classrooms, I was mouthy, I was passionate, and I loved a good argument against authority, especially if I felt like I was in the right.

This passion led me to run for student body vice president, and then student body president. It proved too difficult to convince my basketball friends to take a break from the games to go vote, and it was even more difficult to get them to understand why I would even want to be in both IB and student council. Some laughed at my audacity to even think I could be in student government. As a defense mechanism I made my whole campaign persona unserious, like it was no big deal if I lost.

I did, both times.

Eighth-grade promotion was a big deal. The day started in a line outside the vice principal's office with dozens of eighth-grade boys vying for assistance in tying our ties. A routine part of promotion day for Mr. Singh, it was also a commentary on the fact that many students, like me, didn't have a father around to tie their ties. Girls wore dresses that were prom or quince ready, some with rented limos ready to take them and their friends to the mall after the ceremony. Parents and family took off from work or called in sick for the big day. Some of my classmates were given major cash. In a gym bursting with balloons, we heard speeches from peers and a special guest speaker. We felt wildly celebrated.

Yes, all this for an event that appears to be a foregone conclusion—all children graduate from eighth grade. But these ceremonies take on heightened importance in schools like mine. Among the parents and grandparents were migrant workers for whom a sixth-grade education, much less eighth, had been unattainable. For the students, a high school diploma was far from a guarantee. For some, eighth grade would be the last time they were publicly celebrated. They would drop out of high school, run into troubles with the law, or meet premature death. The pitfalls were many, from high rates of teen pregnancy to the grim reality that the leading cause of death for young Black and Latino men in my city (and our country) is gun violence. Although I couldn't say why, at the time, I knew not everyone around me would make it.

But I loved my classmates, I loved my school. Even in the dysfunction, I had found rich soil to take root in.

3

SCHOOL DAZE

My mom began to notice my anger.

Part of this was our fraying relationship. As a young, overworked single parent, she was exhausted and anxious, and would lash out verbally and sometimes physically. I would respond that she couldn't talk to me like that, or she shouldn't put her hands on me, and these episodes became more frequent and charged as I grew into adolescence. My mom's focus was to make sure I stayed on the narrow path, as she defined it, and more and more I felt she could be a little heavy-handed.

What my mother saw, though, was a young man with a smart mouth and an attitude problem. She was alarmed that I would not just accept her authority, and that I had a tendency to talk back—attributes she felt were dangerous to have. As a mother to a Black son, I am certain she was fearful that if I didn't learn how to obey, something tragic could happen.

In her sporadic updates to my dad, she decided to share her fears. She accepted the predatory charges imposed by the telecompany to connect to the prison system, and had a conversation with Michael about my attitude. Together my parents decided that I should visit him for the first time since he was arrested. Maybe I needed to talk to a man about the rage that was brewing inside.

He was at Mule Creek State Prison. The inmates of Mule Creek were like a who's who of the nastiest criminals: rapists, serial murderers, necrophiliacs, even a cannibal—inmates who came to euphemistically be called "Sensitive Needs Inmates." Charles Manson was incarcerated at Mule Creek until his death in 2017. The drive only took forty-five minutes, although it felt longer. I wasn't terribly excited and I wasn't all that nervous; I felt nothing, empty, like the monotonous brown fields that decorated most of the drive to the prison. Upon arrival, I'm not sure what I expected, but the unwelcoming concrete building imparted an almost physical heaviness. The guards at intake did not make matters better, treating visitors roughly and eyeing us as if we, too, were criminals, guilty by association to someone with a conviction. The energy of the place, the bare walls, the narrow halls, and the enclosed spaces all triggered my claustrophobia—I had to fight rising panic and urges to leave, even though I knew I wasn't stuck and would be allowed out. All the other visitors were either mothers, girlfriends/wives, or children of the men kept in cages.

When my dad entered the visiting area, he looked different than I had pictured him. I had constructed an image of Michael Tubbs as physically intimidating and as someone frozen in his early twenties and was met with a thirty-year-old man. He looked hardened, thin—though with a hint of levity, as if his incarceration from such a young age had frozen a part of his pre-prison disposition. He looked neither like a super-hero nor a criminal.

He looked a bit like me.

As we embraced for the first time that I could remember, I fought the urge to sob, to cry tears that would speak for the relative silence of the past decade. Instead, I held it together, said the customary, "I miss you too," and settled in for a conversation with this stranger who was my dad.

We started with the basics—my favorite color and his. His favorite basketball team and mine. We were cordial but distant, not broaching the agenda either of us had come into the room with. Then I blurted out the question I had been afraid to ask. "Why are you in here?"

He responded with a lecture about the room we were in, and the system. He said that in some ways this was his fate. He said that the deck was stacked against me, too, because I was from a single-parent home, because he was in prison, and because I was a Black man in America, where the expectation for me was to end up with him or end up dead. Prison or death—the options society had laid out for me. Although he never said it explicitly, I understood even then that his challenge to me, the unasked question that later became my driving force, was: "What are you going to do to make it different for you? To prove them wrong?"

The conversation was heavy, and although I did not like the environment it took place in, I did not want to leave. I liked talking to my dad. Leaving was terrible; around the room, guards had to forcefully drag some inmates away from their loved ones. Babies shrieked. Girlfriends and wives cried. Mothers held practiced, stoic looks. It was terrible. I resolved to never set foot inside a prison again.

As I left, I reconsidered my dad's speech. I was puzzled at his refusal to own his actions, to blame everything on "the system" and the odds stacked against him. Church, school, and my moms all reinforced a message of agency, of pulling myself up by my bootstraps—no excuses.

I rejected the idea that factors outside of my control were destined to ruin my life. I would lean into the power of the individual, to what my moms and pastor told me: "You can do it. You just have to work twice as hard." The fire in me found another log to burn, this time in service of proving my dad's grim prophecy of prison or death wrong.

At Franklin High School I continued in the International Baccalaureate program, and it was the same schizophrenic experience of code-switching between regular public high school life on the one hand and accelerated learning on the other. I became even more adept at navigating divergent worlds and actually won elections for homecoming prince, Black student union president, and student body president.

At the beginning of high school, my best friend, Frank, and I made a pledge to become the first Black males to graduate with the full IB diploma and to be college roommates. Our goal was Howard because his sister went there and the stories she told us made it sound like fun. Frank and I were inseparable, friendly but competitive—I was better in the classroom, and he was taller and stronger. He hit puberty way earlier and was by far the superior athlete and ladies' man. During our sophomore year, however, Frank and I began to drift apart. He wasn't able to compartmentalize problems at home and started to focus less on school and more on girls and weed.

After basketball practice during our sophomore year, he

pulled me aside to let me know that his girlfriend of a couple of months was pregnant. I vowed to help him any way I could, but from that moment the spark of motivation just left him. He dropped out of IB and by the time junior year began we were no longer friends. There wasn't a big fight or even a conversation, it just happened. I was hell-bent on getting into college, down to kick it, but only after I did what I needed to do. He and some of my other friends who dropped out of the IB program after sophomore year felt I thought that I was better than them, that I was too important to hang out.

I had other casual friends and a whole slate of activities to keep me busy, but from then on, I felt isolated and lonely. I enlarged my social circle and became even more friendly with my IB nerds, but I wondered if college would end up being like this: lonely. I worried it would be like the experience I had in my high school classrooms, namely that of being the *Only*, being the *Other*—working incredibly hard for a reward I'd have to trust would appear in the coming years.

The school day began when I boarded the bus at 6:22 A.M., joining the kids rapping Lil Wayne lyrics and arguing over anything and everything, all while imploring the driver to "Turn the heater on." On the bus is where I met Chauncy, who became like a little brother to me. He always had a brush, belt, or lotion ready, as I was sure to forget one of those things in the morning rush.

By 7:00 A.M., we arrived at the table, my hangout spot in the morning where everyone, from jocks, to gangbangers, to IB kids, to security monitors, to cheerleaders, to Science Olympiad members would stop by and say, "What's up, Tubbs?" The table became a watering hole of sorts, an intersection point where all my worlds would collide. One of my friends would call me "the Mayor of Franklin" because, although I didn't feel close to many people, I did make it a point to be coo with everyone.

Like most moderately athletic teenagers, I harbored hoop dreams, so I played basketball my first couple of years in high school. I missed practice a lot, though; I hated conditioning, and my civic commitments were more and more in conflict with our practice schedule. To my undying shame, I wasn't even deemed worthy for a jersey for the freshman team. Sophomore year, I grew to 5'6" and had worked my way up to becoming sixth man. Then the JV coach was replaced with my coach from freshman year. I decided to quit—it was clear I wasn't going to get a scholarship for my hoop prowess, but I was also afraid of going from sixth man to the end of the bench.

I still beat myself up about it. I felt like I hadn't risen to the challenge, like I hadn't proven them wrong. I couldn't stay away from the court for long, however, and spent the rest of high school as the stat boy, traveling with the team when I could and taking down the statistics.

I didn't have a ton of time. For one thing, I decided to get a job. My mom would flare up or lash out when money was particularly tight, and I wanted to help her out so she could focus on my baby brother, Dre. Let's be real, I also wanted to be able to pay for my own prom tickets, designer clothes, college fees, food, etc. So I started pulling shifts at Barnes & Noble.

I had also become more involved in the community. After participating in the Youth Leadership Academy put on by the city, I applied to join the city's Youth Advisory Commission. I was excited to be selected after an interview including city councilmembers. Fresh off my basketball embarrassment, as a new member of the group, I decided to run for chairman. I rallied all the new commissioners to my aid and, to the surprise of our advisor, won as a high school freshman—chairpersons were always upperclassmen. Part of my role was to meet with the mayor and the city council about the needs of youth in the community and to attend and speak at Stockton City Council meetings. Those nights I set aside my usual wardrobe of saggy pants and tall tees and Jordans and instead donned a suit and tucked in my shirt (still with Jordans). I was often the only teenager, and sometimes the only person of color, debating and discussing city ordinances and programs. I always marveled at how ordinary the decision makers were, how they weren't that much smarter than me as a teen or as anyone else in the community I came in contact with. Still, they had both access and power. Their voices mattered. They made decisions that we were all forced to live with.

When I wasn't the only teen at these meetings, the other was Lange Luntao.

Lange was also interested in city government and in having the leadership positions necessary to be competitive for college admissions. Unlike me, he had grown up in and attended school in one of the wealthier, gated, mostly white neighborhoods in Stockton. Both his parents had gone to college and were educators. He was preppy. He wore Hollister. But Lange's story was more complicated than that—and in later years I'd come to know and treasure the real Lange—but in these early encounters I felt like we were rivals. As teens we both wore masks, trying to figure out how to be comfortable taking up space in rooms not made for us.

As chair of the Youth Advisory Commission, I met community organizers who were turning their anger at the material conditions in parts of our community into action. Many had been doing this work for decades, hammering away at issues of poverty and exclusion. I marveled at their dynamic speaking, poetic musings, and personal stories of redemption— some having gone from serving time in prison to helping improve the community. They became role models for me and showed me a new side of what it meant to have experienced incarceration.

Just like in middle school, at Franklin I was never accused of talking or "acting white." At the same time, gang members in my neighborhood respected that I was on my own path, and never tried to recruit me or rope me into territorial beefs. Although they were loath to say it, there was some begrudging local pride in me. Sure, I was different, with my talk of meetings and IB work, but I was also familiar—I took the bus, listened to the same music, wore the same shoes.

My teachers, on the other hand, stood squarely between me and my goals.

Most of my classes felt like a war, and it was exhausting. I would regrade my work, comparing the way my papers were scored to my classmates', highlighting discrepancies. When I inevitably found them, I would ask my teacher to explain their grading of my paper based on their rubric. More often than not, I would be successful in earning a more accurate and higher grade. I was adamant about earning as close to straight A's as possible and demanded to be evaluated fairly.

My senior year biology teacher had a helmet called the Retard Helmet that he would make people wear if they asked questions he thought were dumb. He also had a Wall of Shame.

My name was up there for cutting class—that my absences were entirely due to representing the city at leadership conferences, attending scholarship weekends, or going on college visits, he didn't care. In his eyes, I was constantly "out of line." Our relationship became so hostile that I would kick myself out of class to spare us both the trouble. I bristled at the ways he talked about my friends who weren't in IB, saying that they were going to pump my classmates' gas some day or barely make it to community college. I was infuriated when he told my classmates I played my "Black card" to garner scholarships and college admissions. He would claim that assignments for which I had already received grades were missing, and my grade always seemed to go lower around finals time.

He was a bully. We didn't vibe. By my senior year, I'd walk into his class and say, "Give me the assignment and I'll go do it in the library. I don't need to be here."

At the beginning of senior year, one teacher called a meeting with my three mothers to discuss my behavior in her class. When Mom, Nana, and Auntie Tasha showed up, not just the teacher who called the meeting, but all my teachers were in the room. I took notes the whole meeting, recording what was said, a skill I had learned as student body secretary.

"What's going on here?" my mom asked. "I didn't get a call from you, you, you, or you. Just from you. What's the issue?"

"We're concerned about Michael's grades."

Mind you, I had a top 5 percent class rank and some of the highest standardized test scores in the entire school.

"He's going to end up lucky to go to community college if he doesn't change his attitude," was the prediction my biology teacher offered up.

"We know things will be easier for him because he's Black,

with affirmative action and all . . ." said the program director as we began to talk about next steps after high school.

Peals of laughter from my team. "If anything, it'll be harder, and he'll continue to work twice as hard!"

As I watched my mother fight for me in public, I reflected on our still-rocky private relationship. As I turned sixteen and seventeen, she was reminded of the pain of her latter teenaged years and became increasingly paranoid in her efforts to ensure that I wouldn't mortgage my own future. She saw peril in routine things like going over a friend's house for a study group and was suspicious of the late nights I spent doing homework. I would find out later that she secretly followed me to proms and formals and waited in the parking lot to observe my comings and goings.

Back in the meeting, my teachers shifted gears. "Where are you planning on applying?"

I didn't tell them the truth, staying generic and evasive. They already thought I didn't know my place and was too ambitious, and I suspected that some might even sabotage my applications. I didn't see them wishing me well at the schools I was eyeing. Sure enough, trying to be "helpful," they urged me to apply to schools I knew to be less highly regarded than the schools they recommended to white students with lower grades and test scores than mine.

A week before graduation, I filed a formal civil rights complaint with the local NAACP against my biology teacher for racism and discrimination. He hasn't been allowed to teach at our high school since.

During Senior Prank Week, some white friends who were cheerleaders wrote *white girl mob* on a Black cheerleader's car.

That's what they called each other; it wasn't intended as racist, and the Black cheerleader didn't take it as such.

So a friend and I wrote on one of their cars *ATL ho*, a tag popularized by Lil Jon and the Ying Yang twins. A harmless counterprank.

A security monitor didn't see it that way. He came over and said, "Tubbs, erase it now."

"Sure," I said. "I'm happy to erase it, just let them see it real quick."

"I said now," said the security guard, as my friend intervened and began to erase. "No, not you. Tubbs!"

"I'll erase it as soon as they erase 'white girl mob' off the car right next to this one," I said pointing.

"No, you're not telling us how it goes."

I left the encounter annoyed but thinking it was not a big deal, until I was called out of calculus class later that day. I walked into the principal's office to find school district police rolling deep while others took pictures of the car. They were writing a police report, much to the chagrin of the cheerleaders I had pranked, who couldn't believe that harmless fun had escalated to the point of law enforcement involvement. When the district police tried to put me in their cruiser, I went berserk.

"There's no way I'm getting in that car. Call my mom! CALL MY MOM!"

My mom and Nana arrived to campus in record time, confused and trying to calm me down. I explained to them what happened, which fired up my mom for battle, while Nana took on a more strategic demeanor.

Unbeknownst to me, before their arrival the principal had drafted up suspension papers for me for vandalism—a week before college admission decisions were to be released. My co-conspirator, who was white and Asian and who had written on my friend's car with me and supplied me the markers, wasn't charged. Neither were the white cheerleaders who wrote *white girl mob*. If the charges were filed and suspension determined, my college offers would be rescinded. It appeared that they wanted to make an example of me.

I went off. "It's *racist* for the girls to get away with writing *white girl mob* on the cars of Black students! That's literally hate speech!"

To add to the farce of the situation, there on the wall of the principal's office was a sign that read, CONGRATULATIONS MICHAEL TUBBS, WINNER OF THE ALICE WALKER ESSAY CONTEST.

Hundreds of students from all over the Bay Area had entered that essay contest earlier in the year, and I still found it hard to believe that Ms. Walker had chosen my narrative of growing up on the south side of Stockton and the lessons I'd learned from watching both my mom and my dad, as the winning entry. In doing so she validated my story as one that deserved be told, remarking that it embodied the themes of her legendary novel *The Color Purple*.

What happened next was even harder to believe, because the prize for winning the contest was meeting Ms. Walker herself.

Although only seventy miles away from my home, her idyllic residence in Berkeley, California, might as well have been the moon. She had a nicely manicured lawn, imposing steps, serenity in the soundscape, and a mini forest, an abode that looked nothing like the neighborhoods I was familiar with. Accordingly, I gave myself a pep talk as I knocked on her door.

"You are meeting Alice Walker, don't go up here acting like no groupie." I didn't tell Ms. Walker that I planned to send that essay to the colleges I dreamed of attending. I didn't tell Ms. Walker how strongly I identified with Sofia's line, "All my life I had to fight!" I didn't tell Ms. Walker that her essay contest was the first time I had taken the opportunity to mention my father and where he was in public. I just told her thank you, posed for pictures for the *San Francisco Chronicle*, and smiled at my mom and aunt and at a Pulitzer Prize winner with whom I was having a conversation.

Yes, I could finally admit that my anger and my drive were both linked to my experience of having lost someone I cared about to the American penal system. That I had gained so much from my mothers' struggles and my father's absence. I couldn't deny that they were pivotal parts of who I was becoming. I reflected back on the conversation in Mule Creek prison and how it had helped me focus my passion for changing my own life, for defying the odds.

My father has never seen his name, *Michael Tubbs*, on a plaque for a positive achievement. His journey to Mule Creek prison and others like it, however, deserves more explanation.

On February 14, 1996, the day his daughter Mikaela was born, he was let out of prison on an ankle monitor. Mikaela was born with severe birth defects and died shortly after birth. Michael didn't have any savings or income, but wanted to be able to bury his daughter with dignity. He needed four thousand dollars for the funeral.

He pulled up on some guys that he knew were in the drug game and forced them into a car at gunpoint. He drove them to where they stashed their money and he took thirty-seven hundred dollars from them. No one was physically hurt and, again, he figured they weren't the type of guys that would go to law enforcement. He was prepared to live with the consequences of street justice.

With the money, he paid for the funeral. My mom allowed me to attend after I told her that I wanted to go and see my little sister off to heaven. She dressed me in a tiny suit, and I sat next to my father in the limo, quiet and serious.

Weeks went by and my dad thought nothing of the robbery, until the guys he robbed were apprehended by the police. In return for a lighter sentence, they agreed to corroborate and tell of crimes they knew of committed by other people of interest. My father's faith in an "alternative justice system," as it turned out, had been misplaced. On August 14, 1996, he was arrested and charged with a violent crime: kidnapping and robbery.

California's draconian Three Strikes sentencing law had been instituted just two years prior, in 1994. It imposed automatic life sentences for people convicted of certain felony offenses if they already had two convictions on their record. The intention was to create a serious deterrent to potential reoffenders, but, decades and untold amounts of trauma later, there's near universal consensus that Three Strikes was a failed policy that created more harm than good. This "tough on crime" law swept an entire generation of mostly Black and Brown boys into the exploding prison population and rendered the generation after them fatherless. First strikes frequently were for things as frivolous as stealing loose change from a parked car, or even felony vandalism. Because of historic (and continuing) racist profiling, young men of color had more encounters with the police and were therefore the ones more likely to be given strikes. Until a reform of the law in

2012, Black people were twelve times more likely than white people to be incarcerated under Three Strikes in California.

The result was devastated neighborhoods, families like mine broken apart, and gutted household incomes. Meanwhile, the data collected since then shows zero correlation between the drop in crime (which happened nationwide starting in the early 1990s) and the theoretical deterrence of Three Strikes. There are compelling arguments, including from the criminal justice–focused Marshall Project, that the impact of the law was so devastating that reparations should be paid to the men who were sentenced under it.

I was beginning to see that there might be something to what my father had said about a rigged system.

Back in the principal's office, Nana's calm diplomacy prevailed. "He's so sorry," she repeated. "What can he do to make up for it? Maybe he can do a presentation or something about the dangers of vandalism." Soothing, smoothing things over. Nana was from a different generation and had learned that the best way to survive the system was to know when to fight and when to cooperate. Eventually, the principal decided that I would not be suspended and that the school district police should not refer my case over to Stockton PD. There would be no charges.

I should have known that something really great was coming up, because there's a pattern to these things. Before every great victory, there had to be a great attack or fight. It is always the darkest before dawn. Weeping may endure for a night, but a joy comes in the morning. You will reap a harvest if you faint not.

I left Alice Walker's home with a handwritten note that explained why she had chosen my essay to be the winner of her essay contest. Her words remain a reminder and an in-spiration:

> Tubbs' essay exemplifies what *The Color Purple* is about: the belief that each of us has an indomita-ble spirit within us that we can trust to carry us through perils even more terrifying than the sys-tems of domination—whether by race, gender, class or other—set in place to keep us down. That we own our own souls and are therefore offered the freedom to choose dignity and self-respect, which, happily chosen, gives us the courage to live our own lives. And, what is more, to cherish and enjoy them!

4

DREAMS

The chocolate box was copper-gold and tied with a red satin ribbon. I'd seen them before. We had them for sale at the front desk at the Barnes & Noble where I worked. But in Stockton nobody had ever bought one, at least not anyone I rung up. Here on the East Coast, this young Black girl pointed the clerk to the biggest box and laid down her credit card.

"One of those, please," she said.

The clerk didn't raise an eyebrow, just slid that burnished gold box over the counter to her. She paid nonchalantly, we left the store and joined the rest of the group. I couldn't let what I had just witnessed pass.

"You bought that expensive chocolate!"

"What are you talking about, Tubbs?"

"You bought that Godiva chocolate," I said, pronouncing it "Go-DEE-va." I'd never heard anyone say it out loud before, much less buy it, so I gave it my best guess.

Everyone erupted into laughter. "It's *Guh-DIE-vah*, Tubbs. Godiva."

I was in Philadelphia, age sixteen, having just flown across the country for the first time. I had stumbled on the Leadership Education and Development (LEAD) program online: an initiative designed to pipeline minority students into the corporate world. Taking the name at face value, I applied because I was interested in leadership. I was selected as one of thirty students to spend the summer at the Wharton School at the University of Pennsylvania.

I wasn't attending college just yet, my mother reminded me as I prepared to leave. In fact, she said, I was too young to fly across the country alone, so the entire family would be taking a trip to do some sightseeing in Philadelphia. I protested the optics. Surely, they would think, if his family can afford to travel to Pennsylvania, they can afford to pay for him to stay there, I told my mom. They would revoke my financial aid! "You lucky I'm letting you go," was her reply. "Besides, you're not grown, and they don't know what I had to sacrifice to pay for this trip. Plus, I wanna see the country too!"

My mom, auntie, nana, little brother, cousins, and I took that flight together, and on the other side we hailed a taxi to the Penn campus. I became embarrassed when I realized that no one else was moved in with an entourage, not even the students who lived only an hour away. I hurriedly said my good-byes. "It's only a month and a half," I said to my moms as I hurried up the stairs. "It ain't four years, like college."

When I returned to Stockton they told me they had stayed an extra day in Philadelphia after dropping me off, in case I got homesick and wanted to fly back immediately.

The Leadership Education and Development Program, aka LEAD, was my first time outside California, and also my first time being around people of color who weren't all poor or barely middle class. Some of these folks were wealthy, on their way to being the third or fourth generation in their family to be college educated. One student's grandfather founded *Black Enterprise* magazine! It was another world, filled with young men and women whose networks and privilege would put to shame even the doctors' and lawyers' kids with whom I had gone to elementary school. There were times, like the Godeeva incident, when I felt just how far I was from Franklin High School and South Stockton.

I wasn't ashamed of home, though. Whenever I introduced myself, I'd say: "My name is Michael Tubbs and I'm from Stockton (dramatic pause), California." My peers ragged on me for that too. I never heard the end of it: "He's Michael Tubbs from Stockton . . . California." When I walked inside the dorm I always shouted: "Stockton's in the building!" It became so much of my identity that for my birthday they all gave me a signed T-shirt printed with the words STOCKTON'S IN THE BUILDING.

The program itself was intense, but I loved it. Lectures were taught like MBA classes by MBA professors, with cold calling and case studies. We were given team challenges, and I relished presenting our solutions to our professional judges. We also took site visits, which exposed me to another world I never knew existed. We visited Wall Street trading and investment firms, where I learned that tellers weren't the only jobs banks offered. I was amazed at the presenters we had, all Black and Latino, in tailored suits and with elite educations. They talked fast and moved faster as they told us about the business world's cutthroat atmosphere and the need to grow tough skin.

I was lucky enough to be one of just two students in the program on a full ride, and tried to soak everything in. I tried new things like Moroccan food and saw East Coast sites like the Statue of Liberty and the National Mall. Despite the differences between myself and my peers—some of whose parents were VPs at the headquarters we toured—I found community. Unlike at Franklin, I felt able to be fully myself both inside and outside of the classroom. I didn't stand out for being a Black male, I fit in; I didn't stand out for loving education either, among a group all bound for four-year colleges. My professors and lecturers were challenging but generous in their affirmations. I emerged confident: if I had held my own at the Wharton School, hopefully I would be able to hold my own at any college.

I came back to start my senior year raring to prepare for college and reach my full potential.

LEAD poured gasoline on my college ambitions, but it didn't start the fire. That was She-daddy. During the previous school year, she'd had an interview we believed would be our ticket to the middle class, or at least out of being working poor. I made it my personal mission to prepare my mom, and spent hours searching for the "Top 10 Interview Questions" online and we practiced them the entire weekend before her interview. My mom had been at her job as a customer service representative at Health Plan of San Joaquin for six years at that point; she was overdue for this promotion. I had watched her clock extra hours doing health and community outreach on the weekends and knew her stories of people she had trained being given promotional opportunities while she was overlooked. The day of the interview, I was confident that the promotion was hers. She had worked so hard.

The next afternoon, I was puzzled to see her car in the driveway when I arrived home from school. She had only a twenty-minute lunch, from 2:00 to 2:20, so she never came home for it. Inside the house all the lights were off, and I heard muffled crying from her bedroom. My mom didn't cry often, at least not within my earshot, so I hurried back, opened her door, and gave her a hug. "What happened?"

"I didn't get the promotion," she said between sobs.

"What? How? Did they give a reason why?"

"The same reason as ever, because I don't have an associate's degree or a bachelor's degree." My heart dropped, and I looked at the floor. Waves of guilt washed over me. I was the reason she was in this situation. She had planned to attend community college and transfer to a four-year college, but becoming a single parent had made that too hard. Her decision to have me was still impacting her earning potential fifteen years later.

I had begun stammering an apology when she looked up, lifted my chin, and said, "Don't you dare apologize. Instead promise me that you'll never allow yourself to be limited. Promise me that you will get your education. Promise me that if you ever get rejected it is because you weren't the best person, not that you didn't meet the minimum qualifications."

With fifteen-year-old sincerity, I promised. I meant it.

During LEAD I learned that many of my peers were already working on their college applications, complete with expensive test prep classes and admissions consultants. Given the resources present at Franklin High School and my antithetical relationship with many of my teachers, I resolved to master the admissions process myself. I spent countless hours at the Maya Angelou Library reading the *Fiske Guide to Colleges* to develop a list of schools. I saved lunch money for a month and money from my job at Barnes & Noble to buy SAT prep books and AP textbooks. Hours spent on the College Confidential website taught me that the SAT subject tests were more aligned with the AP than the IB curriculum I was enrolled in.

Doing well on standardized tests and mastering the admissions game became my obsession, straining my relationship with my mom and with friends like Frank, who had dropped out of the IB program. My non-IB friends accused me of believing I was better than them because I spent weekends on SAT practice quizzes and lunches catching up on homework. It hurt that they would think that, but I refused to let it deter me. There'll be time to catch up, I would tell them, but my scores have to catch up first.

My mom was a paradox. I knew she was my advocate, but her need for control and her lack of understanding of the college process also led her to be one of my biggest hindrances. We argued incessantly about why it took me so long to do my schoolwork and why more time couldn't be spent on household chores. The stress of raising two Black boys in Stockton, of being a Black woman in America with a low-wage job, of not having time to develop an identity before becoming the caretaker for another human being, would overwhelm her and she'd snap, hitting and yelling at my little brother and me. I took refuge over at my aunt Tasha's until each episode subsided. I ultimately lived half of my senior year at her house.

The night before the SAT was the worst. My mother wanted

the dishes cleaned immediately, but I sharply told her that the test I was studying for was more important than the dishes and I would get to them tomorrow. The argument ended in me being kicked out the house and spending hours at the local park before calling Tasha and asking if I could stay with her. To add insult to injury, the next day I also took the SAT without a scientific calculator—actually, without any calculator, as we couldn't afford one. Needless to say, my math score was terrible.

Through College Confidential, I discovered a program called QuestBridge. It promised to help match low-income students with four-year college scholarships, so in September of my senior year I filled out their application form and settled in to wait the several months it would take to find out if I received one of their College Match Scholarships. QuestBridge seemed tailor-made for me, as LEAD had felt. As my relationships with my mom and my friends were strained, and my relationships with my teachers were antagonistic, it felt more and more like my ticket out of Stockton.

Did u hear about the rose that grew from a crack

in the concrete

Proving nature's laws wrong it learned 2 walk

without having feet

The day of QuestBridge notifications, I was giving a motivational speech and quoting Tupac.

The occasion was not lost on me as I stood looking at the five hundred students of Langston Hughes Academy. Langston Hughes was a public charter school with a diverse student body that was 85 percent Title 1 or living at or near the poverty line. Despite the problems I had with many of my teachers, the principal at Langston had heard of my winning the Alice Walker essay contest and heralded me to his learning community as an exemplary student. I started my speech by admitting that I was not in fact a perfect student, and that I had just as much in common with the kids in detention as I did with the straight-A students. My audience laughed, but I was completely serious. Looking in their eyes I saw the same hunger, the same confusion, and the same questions I knew were in mine: How do we get out of Stockton? Is it possible to make it? Is there something different?

I took a breath and shared with them messages I wished someone had shared with me when I was their age. I told them they weren't crazy to be angry because there were things in their lives that weren't fair. I told them that some of their teachers could actually be racist. I told them that they would have to work twice as hard as others to be successful. And I told them that still, school was more likely to be their way out of poverty than any of the other routes that might entice them. I ended by telling them that, like Tupac, I was crazy enough to believe that roses could grow from concrete. I shared his poem with them, beginning with the lines above and continuing:

> *Funny it seems but by keeping its dreams*
>
> *it learned 2 breathe fresh air*
>
> *Long live the rose that grew from concrete*
>
> *when no one else even cared!*

Be like that rose, I told the kids of Langston Hughes. During the Q and A, one student asked where I was going to go to college. I responded that I was supposed to hear back on that very day. I even pulled out my phone, saying confidently: "We'll find out now!" But there wasn't an email from QuestBridge. No matter—I would hear soon.

The presentation ended with an unexpected offer from the principal: to spend the summer working at the school. It took me seven months to accept the offer, and only because they offered four dollars more an hour than what I was making at Barnes & Noble. That decision would change my life.

The email delay, meanwhile, turned out to be a blessing. The thought had not occurred to me that in applying to some of the most selective schools in the country, rejection was an option. I got the QuestBridge email an hour after my speech, and opened it fully expecting to learn that I was getting a full ride to Stanford, Columbia, or Yale.

I hadn't been matched to a single one of my chosen schools. I hadn't gotten in anywhere. I spent the afternoon telling the students about the rose that "learned to breathe fresh air," and now I felt suffocated. Rejection wasn't supposed to be the moral of the story.

I broke down and cried. My mom called QuestBridge, thinking that there had to have been some sort of mistake. There was none. I was inconsolable.

Fast-forward seven months. I had always spent the night before the first day of school with significant time in front of my closet, not because I had a lot to wear, but because the first day outfit had to be perfect. New shoes and new clothes would only look new for so long, and first impressions set the tone for the year. As I opened my closet that night, however, my aims were different than ever before. I was preparing for my first day as an employee of Langston Hughes Academy, just two weeks after my high school graduation. I wanted to signal a couple of things with my outfit: for the staff to take me seriously as a colleague, and for the students to think I was cool.

Above all, I had to make sure that no one addressing me as "Mr. Tubbs" realized I was only seventeen years old. I decided to wear khakis with my favorite polo, the one that always earned me compliments when I worked the front cash register at Barnes & Noble.

I started at the onset of summer school, which was schoolwide and mandatory. I had been recruited to help challenge the "gifted" students, but as soon as I hit the hallway that first day, I was drawn to the "bad" students: the loud ones, the ones that received a lot of referrals and had a lot of energy. The ones that reminded me of myself, friends at Franklin, family members like my brother and my cousin Donnell. Students like Isaac and Devonte.

Devonte had the raspiest voice, and a worldliness about him that was beyond his years. He was both a joker and a fighter. Although he was intelligent, he lacked a lot of basic academic building blocks and was easily frustrated when concepts would not come to him, which in turn caused him to act out in class. He didn't have a stable home, alternating between living with his grandmother and his aunts. He was unable to talk about his parents without shutting down; a hall aide informed me that his father was incarcerated.

Isaac, meanwhile, was a ball of light and love, with a silliness that bordered on immaturity and masked the dire circumstances in which he lived. He also lived in South Stockton, with three or four generations under one roof. He didn't speak much about his home life and was always hungry. Whenever I had food around, he leaned on my shoulders and begged until it became *our* food. As with Devonte, his intelligence and charisma shone, yet he found school challenging because of a lack of impulse control and because he had never been made to master the fundamentals.

Institutional racism bled into every part of their lives, from the houses they lived in, to the lack of amenities of their neighborhoods, to the health issues in their families. In their stories I saw my own and those of so many of my friends.

A few weeks earlier Frank and I had both left high school with our diplomas, but we had now entered different worlds with vastly different prospects. My stressors that summer were choosing my classes for the fall and buying decorations for my dorm room, while Frank had to worry about whether he would get a call back for a minimum-wage job, and whether, even if he got it, he would make enough to afford baby bottles and Pampers for his now two-year-old child. Being at Langston Hughes allowed me to work off some of my newfound feelings of survivor's guilt.

My only solace was to do whatever I could during that short summer to disrupt the cradle-to-prison pipeline that was my students' lives. I wanted their feelings on their first day of school to be congruent with their feelings on the last day of their high school career: giddy and anxious, all rooted in anticipation for what comes next. For many of my peers, those first-day feelings of excitement and nervousness had become, by the last day, complicated by feelings of fear or dread about a truly uncertain future, having been hemmed in by a limited opportunity structure and the many systematic failures of the days in between.

Over the weeks, my mentoring work grew from a couple

of students to an entire eighth-grade English class. I was asked to cover the class one day for a teacher who was struggling, and one class turned into two, and one day turned into a week, until that became my default assignment. My lessons came not from the standard curriculum, but from the curriculum of our shared experiences. To teach the art of a gripping essay, I used Murphy Lee's song "Wat Da Hook Gon Be?" To teach metaphor and simile I found examples in "Juicy" by the Notorious B.I.G. To teach text analysis we spent a week analyzing the poem I had shared with them during my first visit, Tupac's "The Rose That Grew from Concrete." I marveled at how they readily understood that Tupac was not being literal, but talking about what it takes to grow up under hard circumstances. I had them write their own "rose poems" on how they might grow from the "concrete" in their lives.

Veteran teachers and administrators marveled at how students who underperformed in other classes blossomed in mine. One teacher watched agog as Devonte, who had actually done the reading, became frustrated when I didn't call on him to answer every question. The hall aides were surprised that Isaac was able to sit in his seat for most of the class period and turned off his comedic talent just enough to do some of the work at hand.

Outside my work with the eighth graders, I dropped by to see the sixth graders whenever I could. I often felt like I was in triage mode with the older kids, like in some ways it was already too late. With younger kids, I felt there was still time to shore up their fundamentals and change bad habits. My little brother, Dre, was also in sixth grade, and he ended up attending Langston, so I would stop by his classroom to check on him. While I was there, I'd often see Jesus, too.

On the surface, Jesus did not look like he worked hard or even cared. He didn't take up a lot of space in the classroom. His teacher showed me his work, though, which told the truth: Jesus was brilliant. He had skipped a grade, and was also a great athlete. As I got to know him, I learned that he just did what he was supposed to do. Homework. Basketball. Chores. It appeared to be that simple for him. "He's going to Stanford," his teacher proudly predicted.

I found out that QuestBridge wasn't the be-all and end-all of the college process. Their program only matched a couple of students each year, as it turned out, and those results did not signify anything in terms of actual admissions decisions. Chances of getting in were higher if you applied through the regular admissions process, and for the schools I was targeting, the financial aid would be exactly the same.

For a couple of days after my rejection, I felt like a total failure. Maybe I was reaching too high. Then I got back on the College Confidential forums and found out all of the above.

I engaged other forum posters with all my questions. One poster, Carolyn Lawrence, was actually a professional admissions consultant who typically charged thousands of dollars to help students navigate the process. I don't know if it was my persistence or my personal statement, but Carolyn offered to work with me for free and served as my admissions Sherpa from then on.

"Consider your audience," she suggested for one essay. "Instead of saying 'white people,' say 'the oppressor.'" She also told me to change my email from "lovetob-ball" to something a little more professional. She was a translator of the hidden rules I had no access to because I was a first-generation college student, because my family had meager financial means, and because although I was in an IB program, I still went to a large, underresourced public high school with little experience in preparing students to compete for private school admissions. Resources more privileged students take as a given were, for me, a revelation.

I amazed my senior friends with the same gold mine: I told them about financial aid policies that would make colleges like Stanford and Harvard free for us, about liberal arts colleges, and about how to email the admissions office directly for fee waivers and for applications to college fly-in programs. It is still not clear to me how we expect children to compete equally when the keys to success aren't held by those who need them the most.

Under Carolyn's urging, I applied to fifteen schools. Satisfied, I left one last application open on the computer: the school closest to Stockton: Stanford University. I told my mom that I probably wasn't going to finish the application. There was a question I thought was weird, asking me how I showed "intellectual vitality." "Mom," I said, "I don't know what they mean by that. I don't do puzzles for fun or design experiments. I don't want to go to a school like that. It sounds super nerdy."

"Just do it, Michael. It's your last essay."

"I'm not going there anyway. I'm going to the East Coast for school."

"You're not a quitter. It's one more essay. Just do it."

My mom. She-daddy. My biggest fan, at times my biggest critic. My biggest advocate and occasionally my biggest hurdle.

As Tupac says in "Dear Mama," *And when it seems that I'm hopeless, you say the words that can get me back in focus.*

I checked the mailbox incessantly as Decision Day loomed near. One day, before I could open new letters from USC and American University, sirens filled my ears. The entire block was covered with police cars and a SWAT team was suddenly too close to the mailbox. Police emerged from my neighbor's house with his older brother, Roberto, in handcuffs. He mouthed to me to call his mother, but that message was superseded by officers asking me if I had ever seen him trafficking drugs. I was terrified; I honestly wasn't sure. There was always activity at their house, but at a normal level for any big family in the area. We weren't terribly close, but I knew him as a foul-happy pickup basketball opponent. They led him away handcuffed, and I walked in the house, opened the letters, and found that I had been accepted to both the University of Southern California and American University with full-ride merit scholarships.

Those acceptances were soon joined by rejections from the Ron Brown Scholarship Program, a network of high-achieving Black students I had deeply hoped to join, and a rejection by Duke University, one of my top choices. I was nervous going into the last week of March, when University of California, Stanford University, and Ivy League decisions were to be announced. My mom was more nervous than me. So much so, she borrowed money for my housing deposit down at USC, thinking that it was better to take what was tangible than to lose out if my Ivy League dreams didn't come to fruition.

Before heading to the bus for work at Barnes & Noble on March 30, I checked my email. At the top of my inbox was the subject line: "Your Stanford Admissions Decision." I contemplated reading the email after work, as the rejection that felt imminent would sour my mood and possibly my morale and productivity. Still, I clicked. My eyes darted down through the screen as I held my breath to brace myself for the rejection. I read it. Then reread it, and read it again. And then I laughed and cried. Called my nana, mom, and aunt. Laughed. I ran outside and looked around the neighborhood. Tried to take it all in. It felt like something drastic had happened, and things no longer would be the same. I was accepted into Stanford University. I missed the bus. I was late to work.

My boss at Barnes & Noble was incredulous. "You? Stanford? No way." Here was the bigotry of low expectations I knew from school. She requested that I show her proof that I was accepted on the spot, so I printed the email from her office computer. "Oh. Wow," she mustered up in reply.

The next day my boss's surprise was mirrored by my biology teacher's prognosis, delivered in front of my classmates, that I had played my "Black card" to get into Stanford. His sister, another teacher of mine, went out of her way to make sure that I realized that Stanford was doing me a huge favor and that I would be out of my league there. "You were a big fish in a little pond here, but at Stanford you'll be lucky to even swim."

She went on, "Are you sure you want to major in political science? That might be very hard for you. People with money major in that."

As Pharrell Williams said in "So Ambitious," *The motivation for me, was them telling me what I could not be, oh well.*

* * *

As the summer passed, I began to see the school system in a different light: that of potential. What if the system could be reformed so that students like me could thrive? I spent time with Langston Hughes's principal, talking him into reimagining our detention space as a space for students to reflect and grow. I told the principal how the detention system echoed the school-to-prison pipeline, with students playing the role of the humans locked in cages in our jails and prisons. The detention area itself felt like prison: students were made to sit silently in a windowless room, facing a blank wall. In partnership with the newly hired restorative justice coordinator, we added motivational quotes and color to the room's walls, posed reflection questions for students to respond to, added beanbag chairs and a wellness corner, and even had a little bit of meditation music going. Although meditation was not my personal practice, I saw the value in creating a space for the students to take a time-out but, more importantly, to get in touch with their feelings in a space that felt different from the classroom, but also wasn't a waiting room for institutionalization.

My summer at Langston shifted education, in my mind, from a means to escape Stockton to a way of gaining critical thinking skills and the agency to change the status quo. No wonder I was only now seeing it that way, given how seldom people similar to me had occupied positions of power and agency around me. I had only three Black teachers and one Black male teacher during my entire K–12 education, all in middle school. The only Latino teachers I had were in Spanish. My experience at Langston pointed to the truism that the people in positions of influence and authority mattered, and that if I didn't like something, I would have to roll up my sleeves and change it. I would have to occupy the essential spaces, win the necessary support, and embody the qualities I wanted to see instead.

Summer turned into fall and I had to say my farewells to the student body before I moved to Palo Alto. The cafeteria was packed for the school-wide assembly and all eyes were on me again. I was in the front row, fighting back tears as the students performed songs and speeches they had written and cards they had created to send me off to Stanford. My eighth-grade boys composed a rap/essay with the hook, "What's up Mr. Tubbs? How you doing today? I want you to know I look up to you. It's like you're the one that taught me how to tie my shoe." Emotion got the best of me and my tears flowed freely, as did the tears of many of my students, Isaac and Devonte included.

My experience at Langston Hughes Academy was so trans-formative that I tried to take a gap year to stay longer. All summer I had improved as an educator, but also deepened my emotional investment in my students. The difference I believed I was making—and what it was teaching me—bode well for the school year, I felt, and maybe staying a year would help me change the trajectories of my vulnerable eighth graders. Many of my students also had experiences with abandonment, whether due to incarceration, premature death, or family rupture. Devonte often reminded me of how his dad "left" him and went to jail, particularly after he heard my colleagues asking me about when I was leaving for college. I was aware of the potential of being another disappointment to them.

After explaining that my spot in Stanford was guaran-teed, and that countless students took gap years or deferred admissions, my mom and the Langston Hughes principal still refused to entertain the notion. Mr. Solina was the first school leader I had encountered that was truly student-centric. Although I had zero experience, he took my suggestions seriously and gave me the flexibility to connect, to question, and to grow. As a white man, he worked to be antiracist and pushed all of his staff to make sure our students learned. He was a boss that didn't question whether I had gotten into Stanford, and insisted I take the opportunity immediately—while also asking how often I'd be back.

As I walked out of the cafeteria on my last day, my students in tow and Mr. Solina's last question lingering, I told them through tears that I would find my way back to Langston Hughes and home.

5

HUSTLE AND MOTIVATE

Driving down University Avenue, my little brother, Dre, remarked that there was no trash nor graffiti anywhere. Stanford was so much cleaner than most neighborhoods in Stockton, he meant. When we reached our destination—the parking lot of my freshman dorm, Ujaama—we found that it was barren. Deserted. No one there. It was 3:00 P.M. on move-in day, and I was the last student to arrive.

Despite Stockton being only an hour and a half from Stanford, I dragged my feet on making the move. Over the summer I stewed on the toxic comments from my high school teachers. Even though I knew they were racist, they still got under my skin. I dreaded four more years of microaggressions and loneliness in a majority-white academic setting, and I was battling a strong case of imposter syndrome. I thought everybody at Stanford would be wealthy and otherwise privileged. I was nervous that I wasn't going to succeed academically, that I would be lucky to even graduate. I feared, silently, that there was no place for someone like me there. Although I'd just done everything I could to leave Stockton, it was still home, even the bad parts. Stanford was a big unknown.

Dre had none of my nerves. Looking at the billboards of prominent Stanford students, athletes, inventors, and founders that lined the campus walkways, he remarked, "It's going to be crazy to see one of you up there one day, bro." I smiled, hoping that I was hiding my nervousness at the pressure of expectations from my little brother, the rest of my family, the kids I'd taught over the summer, and myself.

The whole family was in tow. Upon walking through my dorm room door my mom went to work disinfecting everything with Lysol, Nana stood by the bed in the corner, her stoic face betrayed by a shaking knee, and Aunt Tasha began to cry. Together we unpacked suitcases and trash bags full of the clothes, posters, and supplies I had bought with my scholarship and work money, along with just a few mementos. We worked in silence. Looking back, I'm sure my moms were thinking of how quickly the previous eighteen years had passed, of all the sacrifices they'd made. I hope they were thinking that they'd succeeded in what they had set out to do.

We didn't explore the campus that day, just stayed in my dorm room, packing and unpacking, arranging and rearranging. As it grew dark, we walked down to the car and I gave each of my three moms a hug. I did not turn to wave as I walked back to the dorm, alone.

By that time, my classmates had returned from first day activities and had piled into the dining hall to eat. I heard their excited chatter but bypassed it, resisting the urge to cry. Back in my room I ate Cheez-Its for my first collegiate meal. Soon thereafter I met my roommate, went to sleep, and woke up in the Stanford bubble. An entirely new world.

Ujamaa—"Uj," as it is widely known—is the Black dorm on Stanford's campus, where 50 percent of students are of African ancestry, meaning African American or African. The dorm was created as a response to the demands of Black student leaders that "took back the mic" from the university president during a town hall in response to the murder of Dr. Martin Luther King, Jr. I ranked Uj as my top choice for freshman living, as I was hopeful it would be similar to my experience in LEAD. It did not disappoint. One of my resident assistants, Girmay Zahilay, a first-generation college student and president of the Black Student Union, provided an example of social and academic excellence and mentorship that helped ease my nerves.

At the center of Uj was Jan Barker Alexander, Director of the Black House and the dorm's resident fellow. In her first speech to us, she said that there was no prescribed notion as to how to be Black at Stanford, and that to be a Black student at Stanford meant to just be excellent. She told us that Stanford didn't do us any favors by letting us in; rather, that our experiences and intellect were assets the campus needed. All of us freshman residents were walking in a legacy of leadership, she added, and we had a responsibility to continue it.

It was in the halls of Uj that I met Cameron Henry. Slight and dapper, a Renaissance man always ready to rock a bow tie, Cam was from a different planet than the guys I grew up with. He initiated conversation by talking about his love of Chicago, which mirrored my love for Stockton. He did not look or sound like how I envisioned the Chi, but his hometown loyalty was legit. As we talked more, I marveled at his background: the fourth generation of his family to go to college, his father had a Ph.D. in economics from Harvard, and he was Black! Despite our differences, or maybe because of them, we've been best friends ever since.

By the eve of the first day of classes, I was feeling more in my element. Uj was an inspiring place, and I could get along with many of the folks I met. Still, I felt nervous about attending my first Stanford classes. David, my roommate, looked puzzled as he saw the care with which I went through my closet. "There's no dress code here, bro," he said, laughing.

"I don't know how you did it at Sidwell Friends, but this is the chance to make a good impression on them upperclassmen ladies," I shot back. I settled on my Lacoste polo, Air Jordans, and slightly baggy True Religion jeans. The familiar first day of school routine helped ease my anxiety, as did a devotional I read the next morning. The day's Scripture was from the first chapter of the book of Joshua, in which, just before Joshua enters the Promised Land, God gives him an important reminder: "Everywhere your feet walk, I have given to you." It would take time for me to internalize those words, but they would become a mantra by which I would remind myself, whenever I felt out of place, that Stanford was mine, too. Everywhere I walked was mine.

"Clearly, people are poor because they don't work hard enough. Look at all the immigrants that come to this country and make it! We give too many handouts and take away the incentive to work hard!"

I looked around the large lecture hall to verify that I wasn't hearing things. *How the hell can he think that?* I wondered as I waited for someone to challenge the speaker, an upperclassman. Surely, I thought, one of these valedictorians or Mensa members would set him straight. When no one did, I raised my hand and began speaking rapidly, as I do when I'm angry. "I completely disagree. The readings assigned illustrate both the existence of institutionalized racism and that meritocracy is in some cases an illusion. The entire passage we read for class talked about how the SAT is more of a proxy for wealth than achievement or merit. In fact, from experience I can assure you that those who work hardest in our society oftentimes are paid the least!"

My professor of Introduction to Sociology nodded in approval. "Correct, Mr. Tubbs. The readings did say as much."

I was thrilled by this intellectual validation, feeling a rush of belonging. At the same time, I couldn't believe some of the "brightest minds" in the country thought the way that upperclassman did.

Leaving class, I hit up Cameron Henry to vent.

"Breh, these are the people who will make the laws that determine who gets access to resources and who doesn't. Only because they attended Stanford. That's hella messed up!"

"Yeah, man, we have to change that," he agreed. "Maybe that's why we're here."

I learned so much that fall, soaking up theory to make sense of what I had seen growing up. In a class called The Urban Underclass, I was taught the difference between income and wealth, the history of redlining, and the ways in which policies created the environments that made it hard for people to pull themselves up by their bootstraps. In my freshman seminar—Freedom, Equality, and Difference—we grappled with the meaning of justice, of opportunity, and of multiculturalism against the backdrop of President Barack Obama's historic presidential campaign.

The greatest thing about my Stanford classes was that I

was allowed to disagree, even vehemently so. Unlike in high school, debating ideas with peers—and even professors—was not a reason to get sent to the office, but rather a reason to earn the professor's respect and praise. When something didn't make sense or was just jacked up, at least I could say so.

In October of my freshman year, the Palo Alto police chief made a blatant appeal to her officers to racially profile Black men. This was 2008. Barack Obama, a Black man, was the Democratic nominee for president of the United States and had a real chance of winning. Meanwhile, this was happening in my new city. I was indignant and ready to act.

But first I called my mom.

"What does that have to do with you at Stanford, Michael? You just got there," my mom said, a warning in her voice.

I told her I was gathering a bunch of students to go down to the Palo Alto City Council and ask for the police chief to either make changes or resign.

"Michael, please don't cause trouble. You need to focus on school; you only been there for a month, you don't need to make any enemies. What if you get arrested? Michael, please, every fight is not yours!"

We were going to have to agree to disagree. After all, it was from her that I'd first learned to stand my ground when I had been wronged. "Don't let anyone walk over you," she was fond of telling me, whether on the basketball court, in the neighborhood, or in the classroom.

"Okay, Mom."

"Michael, I'm serious. I know you are going to do what you want to do, but listen to me."

"Okay, Mom, I gotta go! I'll talk to you next week."

I headed to the planning meeting I had called for the protest. As I laid everything out, some of the seniors in the Black Student Union looked at me, this little eighteen-year-old freshman, like: *What are you talking about, child?* But I knew about city council meetings from Stockton. I knew there would be a section for public comment in this one, and that would be our chance. I convinced fifty students from Stanford to attend the Palo Alto City Council meeting with me on the night of November 3, 2008.

I was our closing speaker at the meeting and articulated our demands. I concluded by remarking on the irony of having this discussion the day before the presidential election and said that I was "excited about working with the Palo Alto community to make sure racial profiling doesn't exist in any way, shape, or form."

The police chief resigned soon thereafter.

Following that meeting, I co-founded with other student leaders a taskforce to end racial profiling in Palo Alto. I was still learning how to get to class every day without getting lost, but people suddenly saw me as the leader of a movement on campus. Students began to send me emails about negative experiences they'd had with Palo Alto PD, asking me to use them however would be helpful.

Our meetings with the city manager and the police department were tense, studded with their adamant claims that they were not racist. To lighten the mood, when a police officer group challenged us to place ourselves in an officer's shoes, I quipped, "We should do a ride along together, it could be the 2008 Freedom Ride!" Before we adjourned I always asked simple, direct questions: *By when?* By when would they do what they had promised?

The city manager shook his head at me with a slight smile as we exited one meeting, saying, "I see why you're here—you ask the tough questions."

When I called my mom to report on our progress, she responded with a sigh that did not hide the smile in her voice.

"Okay. Just make sure you graduate."

"Robert L. Hayes, and this is my wife, Georgia," I said with my best rendition of a southern drawl. I was one of the lead actors in the play *The Exonerated*, playing a man wrongly accused and on death row in Florida.

Stanford allowed me to try new things, and I did so with gusto. Alongside my police reform work, I squeezed in time to join the debate team, emcee the freshman talent show, and intern for the student government and the NAACP. Then there was theater. I had always wanted to act, but the plays in my high school didn't speak to me like the student-produced plays at Stanford did. When I started *The Exonerated*, I actually supported capital punishment, but after delivering a monologue before my character's wrongful execution and reading the research that accompanied the play, I became a staunch opponent and even led anti–death penalty protests on campus. In the audience of every play I did, of course, my mothers were front and center.

As I branched out, Ujaama never stopped being my home and safe place. This was largely due to Jan Barker Alexander, our community's matriarch and increasingly my own biggest influence at Stanford. Just 5'2" but looming large, Jan reminded me of the strong women that had dropped me off at Stanford for my education. I would routinely find myself in her cottage working through new challenges to my precon-

ceived notions, particularly around class and sexual orientation. During the discussion around Proposition 8, I told her
I was surprised that so many Black students were in support
of gay marriage, and she smiled and told me that she was
excited to see the ways in which Stanford would help expand
my thinking.

She was also one of my few mentors who was supportive
when I decided not to run for campus senate after I had garnered the most signatures of anyone planning to run. The
Associated Students of Stanford University, or ASSU, is the
student governing body composed of fifteen students between
their sophomore and senior years. The biggest job of the senate
was appropriating student fees to programs, and there was always strong representation from Ujaama and the Black Student
Union in student government. I wanted to continue the legacy
of leadership I had heard so much about and figured that being
an undergraduate senator was the best way to do that. After
receiving the most petition signatures, however, I changed my
mind. I found another way in which to make an impact.

"Mr. Tubbs is here!" "Yo what's up, Mr. Tubbs!"

I was back in the hallway of Langston Hughes, greeted with
the familiar chorus, along with smiles and hugs and a couple
of headlocks. Langston Hughes was my first stop during my
first collegiate spring break, and as soon as I pulled into the
parking lot I was reminded of the deep love for teaching I
had found the previous summer. As I checked in with my former students, I was disappointed to see that the gains of the
summer hadn't been maintained with those I spent the most
time with, like Isaac and Devonte. Their improvements were
marginal at best, although they did their best to convince me

otherwise as I grilled them about their grades and classroom behaviors. Teachers agreed that even though their attitudes had changed, the daily discipline needed to stay successful in the classroom was elusive for them.

The hour I had scheduled at Langston Hughes turned into four, as I caught up with old colleagues, played basketball at lunch, and sat in my old classroom answering myriad questions about Stanford. My collegiate life felt distant. Here I felt rested and rooted. As thrilling as it was to be a college student, I realized I had never felt more accomplished than when helping the students in my community to see themselves as college students. When I finally took my leave of Langston Hughes, I felt guilty knowing that I was going back to safe, clean spaces and almost unlimited resources, having told my students to work toward academic success in a place that was in many respects the opposite. I resolved that I would find a way to make working with students part of my time at Stanford.

Back on campus, current student senators told me I'd need to choose between Stanford student government and tutoring. I couldn't do both. Surprising many of the student leaders, I decided to drop out of the senate race. I didn't want to disappoint the people who had supported my nascent campaign, but I felt sure of my decision. Before spring break, campus politics had seemed like an exciting next step, a way to broaden my horizons and become a leader while seeking a new platform to express my convictions. Now, I realized I didn't think it would be a good use of time to make Stanford students' experiences even more enjoyable, when I could work to make sure students in neighboring communities got the opportunity to attend Stanford. I didn't feel a connection to politics if it made no tangible impact on those I wanted to help the most.

During my freshman year, I met mentors like professors Gary Segura, in an American politics seminar, H. Samy Alim in a hip hop education class, and Prudence Carter in an urban education course. They all challenged me intellectually, taught me how to marry the theory I was learning with the reality I had observed growing up, and pushed me to be an "organic intellectual," someone who would take all I was learning and make it accessible to the communities I came from. It was energizing to see younger people of color as tenured professors at Stanford, as most of my educators in high school were not. I was most excited to take African American history with Clayborne Carson, the nation's foremost expert on Dr. King and the director of the King Papers Project. In his course, I read Dr. King's *Where Do We Go from Here: Chaos or Community?* and was struck by his support of a universal basic income in the text. That freshman fall I grappled with the efficacy of the idea, and told myself that it would be cool one day to be part of a conversation about the Poor People's Campaign and this unrealized aspect of Dr. King's dream.

"When something is in your heart, Michael, do it," Jan Barker Alexander told me when I said I wanted to engage with the community instead of entering the senate race. I had expected a different reaction, since a big part of being a senator was to advocate for community centers like the Black House and dorms like Ujaama. Here I was telling the leader of both that I wouldn't be in the student senate, protecting the funding and recognition of the Black community at Stanford. But Jan thought bigger, and she thought of me. I was caught off guard as she continued, "Trust yourself. It's gotten you this far."

Instead of serving as a student senator, I took a job with Stanford College Prep to serve as a mentor coordinator, designing and running an after-school program for underprivileged students in East Palo Alto. Later that spring I founded the Phoenix Scholars, which paired mentors with high school seniors from low-income families to help them navigate the college and scholarship application process. The mentors were Stanford undergrads, many of them first-generation college attendees who were low-income, underrepresented minority students themselves.

Phoenix Scholars began as a class paper on access to higher education. In the course of research, I discovered data that mirrored what I had observed at my high school—that just 8 percent of students from low-income households graduate from college by the age of twenty-four, and only 3 percent of students at the nation's top 146 colleges come from the lowest income quartile. I learned that low-income students don't apply to selective universities because they (falsely) believe they are academically and financially unqualified, or are told this by school authority figures, as I was. The studies I found emphasized the power of college counseling to help students succeed in the admissions process, while documenting how understaffed many high school guidance departments are, frequently only having one counselor per several hundred students.

I created Phoenix Scholars in hopes that other students like me wouldn't be dissuaded from applying to top schools because they thought they weren't worthy, or couldn't afford it, or didn't know where to begin. I wanted to spare others the devastation I felt after I didn't gain acceptance via Quest-Bridge, before I learned that there were other (better) ways to get accepted and funded. I hoped I could offer what my college advisor had provided for me, and what I wished I could provide for all the kids at Langston Hughes. I also knew there were always Stanford students looking for a way to give back.

The program launched at the end of my freshman year, with forty-five mentors and ninety students, for a 1:2 mentor-to-student ratio. One hundred percent of the participants would be accepted into college and three students even earned admission to Stanford. In the decade since that first year (at the time of this writing), 100 percent of the several hundred students mentored each year have matriculated at college, the vast majority being the first in their families to do so. Phoenix Scholars alumni have Stanford, Cal, and Harvard degrees, and have continued to run the organization, extending the ladder of opportunity and upward mobility.

At the end of my freshman year, I was selected "Freshman of the Year" by the Black Community Services Center. Rooted both in Stockton and now at Stanford, I had the foundation to grow from and learn more about everything and everywhere I wanted.

ABOVE: My nana, Barbara Nicholson, and me as a baby (courtesy of Tasha Dixon)

LEFT: She-daddy, aka my mom, aka Racole Dixon, and me at five years old (courtesy of Racole Dixon)

My father,
Michael Tubbs,
and me as a baby
(courtesy of Racole Dixon)

Speaking at church as a child
(courtesy of Tasha Dixon)

LEFT: My hoop dreams were short-lived: posing for my recreation league team at age seven
(courtesy of Racole Dixon)

BELOW: Speaking with Valerie Jarrett after her university lecture during my sophomore year at Stanford

Me with one of my mentors, Jan Barker Alexander,
at the Black Community Services Center award
ceremony during my senior year at Stanford

The result of Oprah saying, "Councilman Tubbs, let's get a picture!" during spring of my senior year

My three moms onstage with me at Stanford's Black Graduation
(courtesy of Rebekah Lucien)

Date with my partner, Anna, in Napa Valley
(courtesy of Anna Malaika Tubbs)

My campaign for city council kickoff at the Van Buskirk Community Center

My mom watches on during my campaign for city council kickoff

Working with Nicholas Hatten during the Get Out
the Vote weekend of my campaign for city council

My right-hand man, Cameron Henry,
and I share a moment before my speech
at my mayoral campaign kickoff

Meeting with my father two
weeks before I announced my
campaign for mayor in 2016

Nana swearing me in as mayor while Anna (left), my mom, Aunt Tasha, and Papa (between Aunt Tasha and Nana) look on

The marquee at Bob Hope Theatre for the swearing-in
ceremony for me and my council colleagues

Multitasking at the dais while mayor of the City of Stockton
(courtesy of Daniel Lopez)

Picture with Stockton police chief Eric Jones
during my first year as mayor
(courtesy of Daniel Lopez)

With one of my co-best men, Lange Luntao,
at my wedding in Cartagena, Colombia

Speaking to Stockton middle schoolers while mayor
(courtesy of Daniel Lopez)

Speaking with mothers and children impacted by gun violence
(courtesy of Daniel Lopez)

A rare moment seated at my desk in city hall
(courtesy of Marc Levin)

Family portrait 2010 (from left, back): Me; my mom;
my aunt Tasha; my cousin Scharlyce; my little brother,
Dre; Papa; Nana; and my cousin Shaleeka

Family portrait 2020: My partner, Anna, and
our first child, Michael Malakai Tubbs, Jr.

6

BOY MEETS WORLD

I refused to use the bathroom at night. There were dogs seemingly everywhere, strictly for use as security, not companions. It was pitch black, no electricity. There was also no bathroom, just a hole in the mud under a tree. For an entire week I did not relieve myself after the 5:00 P.M. sunset—though after a few days, this began to seem a small price to pay for the experience I was having.

On my first night with my host family in El Salvador, they served me beef, sat at the table, smiled, and watched me eat. Famished from the long flight, I dove in before remembering my manners. Had they eaten already? I asked. "We only serve *vaca* for very special occasions, and there's not enough for all of us. Besides we are fasting to raise money for Haiti. The whole village is." Haiti had just been devastated by an earthquake and people around the world were raising funds for their relief, but this family's sacrifice made me stop mid-chew. I couldn't imagine that there were places in much worse condition than this village, yet its people were giving of the little they had to support others. They gave me their most honored meal and did not even get to enjoy it with me.

During the spring break of my sophomore year, I traveled outside the United States for the first time. Instead of the rite-of-passage trip to Cancun, I went with a group to El Salvador to commemorate the thirtieth anniversary of Archbishop Oscar Romero's assassination. It was the first of two trips during college that would fundamentally change how I looked at myself, my communities, and my place in the world.

The El Salvador trip was focused on social justice and liberation theology. I had learned at Stanford that the Christianity on which I had been brought up, a faith that was inclusive and tolerant, was not what many of my classmates viewed as the Christian faith. Their definition of Christianity was far right wing, reactionary, and firmly on the side of God-ordained oppression. The trip included a class about liberation theology, my theology, and I was excited at the opportunity to deepen my faith while traveling with a purpose: to learn about the work and life of Archbishop Romero and to stand in solidarity with those calling for a more just world.

The poverty I saw in rural El Salvador was not comparable to the urban poverty I knew. I had never before seen an inhabited place with no electricity or running water or plumbing. There was just no infrastructure. Seeing this, I felt I understood why my host family had no qualms about Henry, their twelve-year-old son and my local guide, potentially crossing the borders by himself in hopes of some semblance of opportunity.

Children like Henry had to walk miles to get to school, and the nearest school was minimal, to put it gently. Although I spoke virtually no Spanish I managed to connect with Henry and his peers by humming and singing Michael Jackson songs. As a Black American I was already a curiosity and became like the Pied Piper. "Obama!" they called me, or "Michael Jackson!" when they learned that my name was actually Michael. They showed me their community through their eyes. I marveled at their spirit as they showed me the well the community was digging to bring running water to the village.

They also showed me a shed full of baseball bats and gloves. I didn't understand at first, but then Henry and his family told me that every year the Stanford delegation had brought these bats and gloves as gifts. The shed was full because the kids didn't play baseball.

They played soccer. No one had asked the best way to assist the village, or even what activities the children enjoyed doing. No one had taken the time to observe the games the children played. I wasn't surprised, sadly, because I'd already seen our delegation's hubris on display. During a church service, the village priest preached from Matthew 6:3: *"But when you give to the needy, do not let your left hand know what your right hand is doing, so that your giving may be in secret. Then your Father, who sees what is done in secret, will reward you."* Immediately thereafter, our trip leader made a big show of presenting the baseball bats and gloves we were once again bequeathing to the village.

It wasn't only our poor judgment I saw in El Salvador. My time there was the first I learned of America's complicity in the corruption, violence, and economic deprivation in other places. It was heart-opening.

El Salvador in the late 1970s had been plagued by extreme wealth inequality. *Las catorce familias*—"the Fourteen

Families"—controlled the great majority of the country's wealth and land. Over decades, they used the military to maintain power, brutally slaughtering anyone who challenged them. By the 1970s their opposition had organized into guerilla forces that took on the regime's brutal National Guard, which kidnapped, tortured, and killed "subversives," including children and youth, nuns and priests, and the poor. By accusing the opposition of creating a communist uprising, the military regime won the backing of the United States.

Archbishop Oscar Romero was a voice for the voiceless, using his services each week to call out the names of the disappeared and the dead, conducting investigations of human rights abuses, and begging the military forces to disobey their orders and stop the killings. He openly denounced the violence on both sides.

The transistor radio was his Twitter. His sermons were broadcast live every Sunday, and almost every home in the country tuned in to listen.

"The true liberation of our people is found," Romero said in a service during Lent not long before he was assassinated, "in teaching them that there is a struggle between the powers of the earth which trample upon the dignity of the human person and their human rights and that establish political systems that deaden the consciences of those who are powerful. Woe to the powerful . . . when they try to subjugate people to their power by torturing, by killing, by massacring!"

Toward the end of the sermon, he called out the U.S. government by name: "I reaffirm my desire to see the economic support of the United States given to the people of El Salvador without limiting the legitimate right of the people to determine their destiny. As long as this right is not guaranteed and as long as there are no guarantees that this assistance will not be used to repress the people, then it is neither just nor right that assistance from any nation should be provided to our government."

On March 24, 1980, Romero was gunned down at the altar by a death squad of the regime. His death sent the country into a full-out civil war, which over the next twelve years resulted in the deaths of more than seventy-five thousand civilians. The first shots were fired during Romero's funeral, when snipers shot into the crowd of 250,000 that had assembled to mourn his passing.

During freshman year, when my peers were making plans to study abroad, I hadn't had any interest. I was American, focused on American issues and American policies, I said. Now I saw that to actually understand my country was to understand its impact everywhere.

The flip side of these dark revelations about American intervention was, for me, a new understanding of faith in action.

One month before his murder, in an eerie echo of Dr. Martin Luther King, Jr.'s "Mountaintop" speech, Romero had told his congregation: "I received notice that I'm on the list of those who are to be eliminated next week. But let it be known that no one can any longer kill the voice of justice." Dr. King, in what would be his final speech, had said: "I may not get there with you. But I want you to know, tonight, that we, as a people, will *get* to the Promised Land!"

Although Romero didn't formally identify with liberation theology, its spirit was reflected in his life's work to reinstate dignity for the poor and to speak out against their oppression. Liberation theologians believed that the Church needed to engage in *action*—not just words—to push for fundamental political and structural changes that would eradicate poverty. Some of them believed that it was even the Church's role to support armed struggles against the oppressors.

Learning this history gave me a term for the faith I grew up with. This was the strain of Christianity I had learned from my grandma, who was much more about action than words.

From the time I was three years old until I was thirteen or fourteen, Nana took in foster kids, and she raised them like they were my cousins. Usually, she took on the most difficult cases that other folks wouldn't take: kids with behavioral problems, or teenage mothers with their children, and the like.

She spent her whole working life as a case manager for people on welfare, helping them to find work. She chose to leave her government office and set up shop in the middle of the community, regardless of the safety concerns, so that she was more accessible to the people she served. The community center where she made her new office was on a busy thoroughfare called Airport Way, near a bus station and across from a liquor store called New Grand Save. Drugs were trafficked there, and there were a lot of shootings and homicides. In the span of a decade, eight murders happened at that liquor store.

Every month Nana took us to the convalescent homes to be with the old folks: sing to them, talk with them, pray with them. Once I got over the smell—and my fear that they'd never let me go from one of their death-grip hugs—I enjoyed myself. Service was so ingrained in our family that I didn't know there was a name for it. You just did it. When I got to college, I was incredulous that there were programs specifically to encourage students to do "community service." I guess they hadn't grown up with a nana like mine.

Ultimately, what I discovered in El Salvador was common ground. I loved the defamiliarizing experience of seeing geographical and cultural differences and realizing within just a few days how much was shared despite them. A Latin American archbishop, and my hero, Dr. King, preaching the same messages of social justice. My nana serving her community, and my host family raising money for Haiti. In all of it I saw the indomitable nature of the human will and ordinary people summoning superhuman strength to change their world.

After El Salvador I knew I wanted another outside perspective on home. I decided to study abroad in Cape Town, South Africa, during the next school year—not just for a week, but several months.

In advance I spent months studying South Africa's transition from white supremacist apartheid rule to the first free elections that brought Nelson Mandela and the African National Congress (ANC) party to power in 1994. I admired the national constitution, which the ANC crowdsourced before that was a term, receiving an astounding 1.7 million submissions from the public. It contains the most extensive human rights protections of any constitution in the world, including the rights to housing, to assembly and demonstration, to freedom of movement and residence, to labor relations, and to dignity. I fantasized that just stepping foot on the African continent might connect me to some deep sense of self that the transatlantic slave trade had robbed me of. The Motherland.

Nothing prepared me for what I actually encountered in South Africa. I arrived in Cape Town almost exactly twenty years to the day Mandela was released after his twenty-seven years in prison, the day on which he made his famous freedom speech: "We call on our white compatriots to join us in the shaping of a new South Africa." I was excited to see what had been accomplished in the "rainbow nation" in twenty years.

My rude awakening began upon departing the airport. The first thing I noticed on the drive to Cape Town was the townships tucked away on the city's outskirts. They seemed to be strategically placed to remain out of sight of the fine dining restaurants and fancy villas of downtown Cape Town. It brought to mind Tupac's analysis of urban America in his Christmas interview with MTV, when he spoke about Blacks living in an "outer city" of the American psyche.

It was also an omen of a difficult lesson I would learn about making change: progress is often far from perfection.

"He who wants to bring about change must first be changed by those he wants to help," read the door of Beth Uriel, which means "House of Light" in Hebrew. It was a shelter for sixteen- to twenty-four-year-old men who had previously been street children, and the site of my local community service placement. Though only a twenty-minute walk from the houses Stanford owned for students to live in, it was in a world far from the comfort and relative luxury of the collegiate study-abroad experience, which was complete with cooks and domestic help. My assigned job from *Magogo*, the house mother, was to simply build relationships with the shelter residents during my time there.

The guys weren't used to seeing a Black person in a position of authority at Beth Uriel, so initially they thought I was seeking refuge. Once they learned that I was an American college student, I became their only "brother" on staff, and they opened up to me in ways that they refused to do with other employees. We spent countless hours in conversation as they told me harrowing tales of life as street children. Manino had fled extreme poverty in Mozambique, traveling with strangers and then alone, and hustled his way through the streets of Cape Town. Brian had fled the violence of his home in the townships, only to end up in a gang and constant gang warfare. Hour after hour, day after day, I was confronted with stories like theirs.

The young men of Beth Uriel refused to allow me to feel sorry for them or to see them as victims. Instead, they stressed their agency, their ability, the fact that they were alive to share their story. They reminded me often that, rather than feeling bad, what I could do was to help them pass their exams so they could graduate, to make sure there was room at Stanford for them when they were ready to come to America, to attend their rap performances and help them go viral. They taught me, much like Alice Walker had, that there was power in owning your story. That in sharing theirs, they weren't giving sob stories, but rather survivor tales. Through their stories they marshalled the strength to persist.

I asked them why so many of Cape Town's street children were addicted to drugs and they told me that addictions started as inhaling fumes at night to keep warm and help with sleep, which often led to daytime habits and then to harder drugs. They told me how the lice so consumed their bodies that they inhaled so that they didn't itch anymore. They told me about how rich older white people—Western tourists as well as South Africans—coerced them with money to have sex with them and gave them drugs so that they were able to serve as sex slaves for hours. They showed me the scars left by the billy clubs of policemen that drugs helped soothe.

I was embarrassed at the naïveté of my question and the assumptions that had underlain it. Of course, there were reasons for drug use beyond the choices these children were making. Obviously, their addiction wasn't the cause of their homelessness. Of course, for complex problems, things would be much more nuanced than they seemed. I had thought I knew a little about poverty, but much like in El Salvador, generous storytellers showed me the global dimensions of the problems I'd seen at home. I thought I was going to make an impact on the men of Beth Uriel, but over the course of our conversations, it was they who changed me.

The gulf between my time at the shelter and my classes and leisure time was vast. Soon after I started at Beth Uriel, I went with some classmates in a cable car to the top of Table Mountain to catch the sunset. *I have been to the mountaintop!*, I thought as I basked in the surreal beauty of the coastline.

Yet even there, the study in brutal contrast continued. In view was Robben Island, South Africa's version of Alcatraz, where Mandela, Robert Sobukwe, and countless others were imprisoned and forced to labor in a limestone quarry. And there below me were the Cape Flats, the vast flat and dusty "dumping grounds" of the city, where millions of Black and "coloured" (a person of mixed ancestry—African, Asian, and European) people lived side by side like sardines, in shacks made of scraps of corrugated metal, cargo pallets, plywood, and plastic sheeting. One of the Black townships in the Cape Flats, Khayelitsha, was home to between 400,000 and 750,000 people, half of whom lived below the poverty line. There was little to no infrastructure. Many people accessed electricity illegally and shared communal water taps and overflowing pit latrines.

The statistics behind what I was seeing were sobering. The

contrast between rich and poor was immense, I learned, and the wealth divide unequivocally followed racial lines, so that economic apartheid (the word literally means separation—*apartness*) continued even as political apartheid had officially ended. There had been progress: life in the aggregate had gotten better, and between 1996 and 2008 the average income for Black South Africans had more than tripled. A couple of million of so-called "black diamonds" had made it into an emerging Black middle class. But in that same period the average income of white South Africans had also risen and was still seven times higher than the average Black income. Only a quarter of South Africans lived in shacks or mud huts now, as opposed to one-third in 1996. But a quarter of 51 million people is still almost 13 million people.

Violence was also rampant: 50 murders, 330 armed robberies, 550 violent assaults, and 100 rapes were being recorded every day—with the sexual violence vastly underreported: it was more like a rape every seven seconds, many claimed. Like in the United States, tougher sentencing and aggressive policing had been the central strategies to combat crime. Five hundred sixty-eight people were shot dead by police in 2008–2009. Between 2000 and 2010, life sentences increased by 572 percent.

I'm embarrassed to admit that I only drove past most of the townships, which were deemed by the Stanford program too dangerous for us to enter, but I did visit Gugulethu. I had become more accustomed to the push-pull of contradictory feelings that South Africa gave rise to inside my heart. On the one hand, it made me deeply uncomfortable to participate in "poverty tourism," to be part of a group of privileged foreigners who snapped photos of abject misery that was "picturesque."

On the other hand, the local people I met were proud, strong, and generous.

In Gugulethu we ate at Mzoli's, a butcher that offered a *braai*, a unique South African barbeque experience complete with live music, sort of a community center and nightclub. Immediately I was made to feel welcome. The walls that strangers usually erect with others were nonexistent there. Everyone shared their food and their jokes. I was invited to homes, to birthday parties, on road trips. When the marching band started up, I joined it, dancing and drumming.

Life in the township felt vibrant. I met a woman who had a thriving business as a seamstress and was teaching others to sew, refusing to let her HIV-positive status define her. A woman named Mama Vicki had opened a bed-and-breakfast to give visitors the "ultimate township experience." Lwazi Primary School, built atop a rubbish dump with containers for classrooms—used as a set in the Clint Eastwood film *Invictus*, starring Morgan Freeman as Nelson Mandela—had won local, regional, and national soccer tournaments. As Mama Vicki said, "There is life in the townships!" People weren't just waiting for the government to fix things. Statistics about unemployment, poverty, and violence were telling an incomplete story, the locals said.

They were the living embodiment of *Ubuntu*. A cherished concept in the South African Zulu language, I'd first learned the term in high school, and felt it embodied the faith tradition I grew up in: namely the idea that the "We" comes before the "Me," that I am only when you are. I don't become fully human nor come into being until you are fully human and have come into your full potential. It's the closest thing I've found that echoes Jesus' ethos to "do unto others as you would have them do unto you" and to "love your neighbor as yourself." The people of Gugulethu were making a life together, claiming space and dignity in spite of all their challenges.

Being in Cape Town twenty-plus years after the end of apartheid, I realized, was like being in Alabama or Mississippi in mid-1980s America, in the heart of the Reagan Revolution, disinvestment in social services, and the war on drugs. On the way to class, I had a conversation with an Indian man who had been out of work for three weeks and put my time in Cape Town in context and perspective. When I told him I was American, he asked me if it was true that America was a place where everyone has jobs. I told him that in some segments of the African American population unemployment hovered around 30 to 40 percent, and that there were places in the United States similar in terms of development to the townships. We talked about local crime and he remarked that the government shouldn't be surprised it was up when so many people couldn't eat. Nodding, I told him that we had similar problems in America.

Cape Town provided a space for all of us Stanford students to reflect on race and the legacy of white supremacy. As one of a few Black people in the cohort, and the most social, my room became the de facto red table for the group. Night after night, they came to my room and asked questions about being Black in America. Lubricated with wine, in a place half a world away from our normal contexts, we had deep, long "real talks" deconstructing race. We stayed up all night discussing issues that many of us would never touch in America. When their questions would have been considered offensive back home, here I was able to answer non-confrontationally. One student wanted to know if the reason I didn't smoke weed with him and others was because I didn't want to be a stereotype. "No," I evenly replied, "I just exist in a world where if I am caught smoking, say, in Stockton or outside college, with mostly Black people, I know it could have serious consequences. Have you heard of the war on drugs?" Although exhausting and at times infuriating, these conversations helped me recognize that ignorance (willful or not) helps perpetuate racism in our country, and that mass education, a safe space to ask dumb questions and enter dialogue, is needed.

In the midst of these conversations and experiences, I developed a close friendship with a guy whose path I probably would never have crossed at Stanford. Evan had grown up in a wealthy family in the Pacific Palisades, and we had vastly different social circles, as he was a member of the Kappa Sig fraternity and my fraternity was the Black Student Union. We hit it off because of our love of novel experiences. Driving through Johannesburg on a Stanford-sponsored trip, he backed me up when I asked that we stop the bus so that we could walk the hallowed streets of Soweto instead of driving through them. The trip leader relented and Evan and I walked the neighborhood, stopping in a yard to grab a beer and watch a soccer game with the locals. During a visit to the Apartheid Museum, he found me and gave me a big hug, overcome with emotion over the atrocities he had just witnessed in its exhibits. We talked often about the different worlds that we came from and the need to make things better back home. We also had a lot of fun, even when he had to drag me to events like the horse derby or an electronica concert. We never turned down each other's requests to go down to the bar-filled Long Street at night.

Long Street was another study in contrasts. The street's

nightclubs were popular with tourists, including my class-mates and me, but outside each I saw the homeless children that my "brothers" at Beth Uriel had been, manning chosen posts all night. I soon developed a relationship with them, ex-changing fist-bumps in greeting. Every time we exited the taxi onto the street, one who I called Little Bro would come up and say, "Big bro, I'm hungry!" and every time I made sure myself or Evan would buy him Nando's Chicken. Armed with his peri peri chicken he would light up and for a second look closer to his actual age of twelve. His thank-yous were complete with "That chicken was good!" and with news of which clubs had the shortest lines.

The aftermath of interactions with Little Bro and the guys at the shelter was still difficult for me. As bright, ambitious, and resilient as they were, as optimistic and creative as I gen-erally considered myself, I could not see a way out of grinding poverty for them. In much of South Africa, the opportunity structure was not only not fair, but practically nonexistent. That made it different from a place like Stockton. You had to work incredibly hard and have a degree of good fortune to open new doors if you came from where I did, but I was living proof that it was possible, even if very difficult. In Cape Town, I could not see a clear way out or up.

Even with all the structural changes made in South Africa, it was apparent to me that many of the young people—who had had no experience of life under apartheid, or barely—felt dis-illusioned, disappointed in their leadership, and betrayed by the ANC. One in five teenagers between the ages of fifteen and seventeen had attempted suicide. High percentages of them struggled with alcoholism. They were looting stores, blocking highways, and attacking police, who, in turn, fought back hard, with rubber bullets, tear gas, water cannons, and even live ammunition. Young people felt trapped, even nihilistic.

As Mandela had acknowledged in his "new South Africa" speech: "The destruction caused by apartheid on our subcontinent is incalculable. The fabric of family life of millions of my people has been shattered. Millions are homeless and unemployed." This reality came to life in my study of Thabo Mbeki, whom I learned about almost by accident when I wandered into a used bookstore near where I was staying and found a book about him. Mbeki had served as the president until 2008, after Mandela stepped down in 1999. Literally born into the liberation movement as the child of two ANC activists, he had pursued his higher education in England and had to learn to be at ease with privilege and to leverage that network to help liberate his people. In him I found an example of putting purpose to privilege and using the ivory tower to become what Italian theorist Antonio Gramski coined "an organic intellectual," someone with an elite education who is still connected to the struggles of the community they came from. Mbeki was a pivotal figure during South Africa's transition to democracy, appeasing secessionist groups like the Zulus and some Afrikaaners. Yet his was also a cautionary tale, particularly his tendency to view everything through a racialized lens. He dismissed valid critiques of his stance on Zimbabwe's leader, Robert Mugabe, and on HIV and AIDS as attempts to discredit African self-determination, with disastrous impacts for his country and for his legacy.

Transitioning the ANC from a liberation army to a governing structure was an enormous task. To me, it was a lesson in expectations as much as it was a portrait of do's and don'ts.

How could any one leader (or two, or three) perfect the governing of a state in which the majority of the population had been disenfranchised for a century? I found myself reminiscing about Cape Town during the disillusionment period that crept in during President Obama's years in office and those that followed America's audacity of hope philosophy after eight years of President Obama being in power. The nation had projected all its hopes (and, among many white citizens, its fears) on one man. And when one man, or woman, is expected to solve issues created by many over more than a century (or two, or three), it's a recipe for disappointment.

I saw myself in a new light while abroad. In Cape Town I came to grips with the fact that I, too, had privilege, at least in the South African context. There I was not an African American; I was an American Black. American first and Black second. My American-ness, and my knowledge of hip hop, made me an object of interest, made me cool, and enabled me to transcend many of the racial stereotypes that poor and marginalized Black Africans could not. My experiences with "coloured" South African people illustrated to me that there was a deep love from them for Black Americans and Black American culture, although they rarely fraternized with Black South Africans. White South Africans loved to seem (or in some cases be) progressive by speaking with and helping Black Americans, while they might never consider speaking a word to a Black South African.

Every two weeks I was given a stipend—a sum greater than the monthly income for most families in the country. I visited vineyards, restaurants, and beaches that many Black South

Africans would only ever experience as domestic workers, security guards, or janitorial staff. I felt guilty experiencing joy and luxury in the midst of so much suffering.

At times, the heaviness of the history, poverty, and injustice surrounding me made it difficult to get out of bed in the morning, much less to enjoy the privileges of being a Stanford student abroad. When this feeling of despair was at its worst, what lifted me out was the sound of children playing. Despite the myriad problems facing them, the kids were laughing and yelling as they played soccer. They were a reminder that there is a future that has not yet succumbed to cynicism.

Joy. Hope against all hope. Child's play. It's the only way to survive a chaotic, beleaguered world, I thought. *The way to battle injustice. The way to not lose your mind. The way to please God, even, because how better to demonstrate faith than to be a child at play in the middle of a war?*

It was far from the experience of Africa I had imagined, but I returned from study abroad with a much more nuanced understanding of myself, the continent, and the difficulties of making change.

7

CAN I LIVE?

November 1, 2010, started like every day had for the previous several weeks: I rose too early for my taste, spent twenty minutes trying to tie a perfect Windsor knot, skipped breakfast, and rushed onto the D.C. Metro to make it to my desk by 7:00 A.M. The desk in question was located in the East Wing of the White House, which in 2010 was not just any White House, but the *Obama* White House.

There can be no overstating the honor it was to be an intern in the White House of the first Black president. I remembered the debates on the streets and in the neighborhoods of South Stockton, the utter disbelief among the marginalized and poor Black people in our hood about the probability of his election.

"There's no way he can win, man, he's Black, there's just no way!" was always the refrain.

On Election Day 2008, I wore my favorite Obama T-shirt—designed by a classmate, it had Obama's face illuminated with rasta colors—and skipped my lectures. I was too nervous to focus on political theory when history was on the line. When President Obama's victory was called, it seemed that the entire campus descended on my dorm, Ujaama. Jan Barker, realizing the probability, had already instructed our RAs to throw a party. Quiet hours were not an option on this night. We stayed up in a state of euphoria, listening to Young Jeezy's "My President is Black" and talking about what this historic achievement meant for us. Cameron was even more over-the-moon than most, as he was from Chicago. My three moms called together to tell me "Congrats"—they knew how much I wanted/needed Obama to win, and were beside themselves anyway. "He really did it," they kept saying. Hanging up, I went back to the party and wept and hugged and danced in equal measure, ecstatic at the shattering of a barrier that many thought would never be broken. Everyone stood up a little taller that night.

Two years later, although the internship routine had become mundane, the fact that I was working in the White House had not lost its novelty. Every morning I pinched myself as I remembered the chance encounter that landed me in the halls of power.

The previous spring, toward the end of my sophomore year, Stanford alumna Valerie Jarrett, senior advisor to the president, had visited the campus and spoken on the importance of public service. After her speech, a more intimate gathering was held by invitation only. Being only a sophomore, I was not invited. Being me, I pestered the student body president until he said I could be the first alternate, on the off chance someone on the invite list dropped out. I had a strong feeling that I was supposed to meet Ms. Jarrett. I couldn't explain it, but I'd had hunches like this before; the stars were aligning for something. The next day I received an email with the invitation to the VIP reception.

I made sure to sit in the front row, dressed in the powder blue shirt that always earned me compliments and excited to learn about how this Black woman made her way to the West Wing. I was struck by her ease and her sense of purpose. She spoke about leaving behind the prestige and good money she'd made at a private law firm. Despite a swank office on the seventy-ninth floor of Chicago's Sears Tower overlooking Lake Michigan, she had been miserable.

"You can't do what everyone else thinks you should do. You have to assess your strengths and weaknesses and passions."

In the public sector, working for Chicago's first Black mayor, Harold Washington, she had found a sense of meaning, of working for something larger than herself. Ms. Jarrett made a career in politics seem desirable, not to mention possible.

During the Q and A, many of my peers used their question as an opportunity to deliver their personal elevator pitch. There were questions that didn't end with a question mark, filled with platitudes meant to convey how smart or talented the speaker was. As I waited my turn, I was cognizant of the fact that Ms. Jarrett was President Obama's mentor. There was nothing I could say or have done as a twenty-year-old that would actually impress her. I simply told Ms. Jarrett that I appreciated her words, said that I would be in the "Stanford in Washington" program in the fall, and proposed that we grab coffee. I had not yet heard back about my application for that program (which offered students the opportunity to live and work in D.C. while taking classes), but I knew that I was supposed to be in the capital.

It did not occur to me that one did not just ask the senior advisor to the president for coffee. Ms. Jarrett smiled and said without hesitation, "Come work in the White House."

I replied that I was actually hoping to work for the Department of Education, to continue my focus on education policy. It was merely the truth, but my lack of enthusiasm—or opportunism—for her offer had other students raising their eyebrows.

Ms. Jarrett told me to talk to her chief of staff, Michael Strautmanis, and pointed to a 6'1" man who had been standing on the edge of the conversation. He and I spent the remainder of the reception talking about sports, politics, how he met the president and First Lady, and Washington D.C. As the reception drew to a close, Ms. Jarrett said, "See you in the White House in the fall."

Six months and countless emails later, I started as a White House intern, working in the Office of Intergovernmental Affairs.

Each morning I nodded to the Secret Service on my way to the Eisenhower Executive Building, passing by hundreds of visitors at the White House gates—people no different than me, who would never have the access I had been granted as much by a stroke of grace as by my own efforts. "Every time you walk inside these gates, think of the people you are taking with you and think of all the people standing at the gates wishing they could get in," First Lady Michelle Obama had told the White House interns. Her words stuck with me, because they spoke to a problem I was driven to solve: the exclusion of far too many citizens from our nation's decision-making process.

My job was to get in early, prepare the relevant news stories for the senior advisors in the president's administration, and stay late compiling the same from the end of the day. The work required the mind-numbing attention to detail that has never been my strong suit. Still, attending meetings with mayors and councilmembers from across the nation made everything worthwhile. Almost on a daily basis I encountered local elected officials who commanded the attention and respect of the executive office because of their passion and vision for their communities. Real government, I saw—the government not of stump speeches, but of day-in, day-out authority—was powered not by ideology, but by people operating with constraints of time, resources, and temperament. And government worked best when its people understood the experiences of those with access to capital and those without. Combining the lessons of my time abroad with what I was seeing in D.C., I decided that government, at its best, invested in all of its people, while also creating the policies and conditions that would allow constituents to upset the setup when it wasn't working.

On the morning of November 1, 2010, I was googling the mayors of the ten largest American cities to prepare my brief when my phone rang. It was my mom. She didn't usually contact me at work; I had made it clear phone calls should be reserved only for emergencies. After checking over my shoulder for any glaring staffers, I answered.

"Hello? Mom?"

The voice on the other end sounded eerily close to tears. The last time I could remember my mom crying—the *only* time, in fact—was when I was in seventh grade and she'd been turned down for the promotion she'd more than deserved, for the third time.

"Mom!" I said again, concern in my voice. I heard her take a deep breath.

"Call me back after work, I don't want to distract you."

I hurried out of the office without an explanation to anyone, the phone pressed to my ear.

"It's okay, Mom, I can talk now," I told her as I reached the relative privacy of the courtyard.

It was my cousin Donnell. He had been at a house party the night before for Halloween and was found lying face down in the driveway. Shot dead.

"I was at the hospital with Trudy. You have never heard cries like a mother's cry for her dead son."

I've always hated Halloween. As a child, the holiday never had much appeal for me, aside from the candy. I had enough everyday fears—barking dogs, feral cats, heights—without adding demons, zombies, and Chucky or the Chupacabra to the mix. Halloween was associated with death, darkness, and a sense of foreboding I could never shake, perhaps because, growing up in Stockton, death already seemed to haunt my city.

I was intimately familiar with the statistics that hung over a young Black male in an urban environment. I had written research papers and scholarship essays about our bleak prospects in my community and across the nation. The pain I felt this time, however, was new. It was angry, raw, helpless; it was intensely personal.

"I ain't got no money, but Imma come home for sure, Mom. When the funeral?"

"Don't worry about us, we'll be all right. You just continue to do your work and make us proud."

My heart dropped as she hung up.

What is the point, God? What is the point of being at the White House and at Stanford if my own family is literally dying back at home? Fury at my futility.

What type of community was it where mothers had to bury their sons?

My tears welled.

But I had to get back into the office. I dried my eyes and put on my game face just like Mom had taught me. *Never let them see you cry.*

For the rest of the morning, I maintained small talk: a debate about the upcoming midterms, the Lakers' prospects for the season. Only when everyone left for lunch did I let down my guard and begin grieving. I hunkered down with my headphones: Bone Thugs-N-Harmony's "Tha Crossroads," T.I.'s "Live in the Sky," and Tupac's "Pour Out Some Liquor." It was easy for the ninety-nine other interns to act like everything was all right because for most them everything truly was. Why did I have to act like everything was all right, to not be a stereotype of a Black guy from an urban community?

I didn't have enough money in my checking account and savings combined to pay for a flight back to Stockton. During the summer I had interned at Google (working in "People Operations"), but I had spent that money buying a transmission for my car and shifting my wardrobe to look the part of a White House intern. Gone were my Jordans, Rocawear, and Coogi, replaced with Ralph Lauren, Calvin Klein, and anything else I could find on clearance at Men's Wearhouse. Asking my family to pay for my flight back home was out of the question, which partly explained my mom's resignation that I would miss the funeral.

Walking back to the Metro on my way home, I began to question everything. I thought of King Solomon writing in the book of Ecclesiastes: *Meaningless! Meaningless! Everything is meaningless!* Solomon had been granted everything: riches, power, wisdom. Yet his pursuit of wisdom had been a form of "chasing after the wind." I felt a wave of the survivor's guilt that had shadowed me since leaving Stockton. I pondered dropping out of the internship and taking a year off from school to spend time with family. Most of the people I cared about were still back home, trapped in a vicious cycle of poverty and violence. My father, the man who shared my name, had been ensnared by the broken justice system. It was one thing, having escaped the issues, to study them from the outside; it would be another thing to live with them daily again.

Later that night, the same day I'd found out about Donnell's death, a friend in my dorm heard about my dilemma and volunteered to pay for my ticket to the funeral. It was uncomfortable relying on the kindness of others, but my accounts didn't allow otherwise. I fought back tears while I packed my bags. I knew I would be asked to eulogize my cousin. I thought back to the last time I'd seen him, at Shaleeka's high school graduation the summer before. I had just started my freshman year at Stanford and Donnell had decided to go back to school and get his GED.

"How's school?"

"Coo. How's everything with you?"

"Solid."

The truth was that I had always envied his having both a mother and a father to see him through Stockton's challenges. We shared a passion for basketball and hip hop, but our interests had otherwise diverged as we grew older. Never in a million years did I think he would be gone so abruptly. He had been a constant, present at birthdays, holidays, and special occasions. He was family.

And now he was gone, and the police didn't even have any leads on the person who had shot him, or why. His death was senseless and meaningless. Anger consumed me.

Arriving at the airport, the sight of my mom's car offered some consolation. Squeezed inside were my aunt Tasha, my grandmother, my cousins Shaleeka and Scharlyce, and my little brother, Drevonte. They were my rock, my squad, still my source of inspiration and strength. The drive home was full of laughs and church gossip. My mom focused on the upcoming family trip to visit the West Wing.

"Tell Michelle and Barack to get ready!"

Shaleeka suggested they all get matching pearls to pay homage to First Lady Obama. As we laughed, I almost forgot that it was a murder and not just my love for my family that brought me home.

But the murder was on everyone's minds. The streets were talking, even as the police still had few leads. Cousins and friends spoke about the desire to get out there and track down the person themselves. Yet we knew it would only exacerbate the problem if someone acted on street intel and proceeded to execute street justice. Instead of one family grieving, there would be two. Retaliation is a never-ending game.

Instead, we kneeled in church and prayed out loud together, pleading with God to give us the peace and the strength to help us bear a senseless tragedy.

The night before the funeral I paced my room, sleepless, trying to figure how to eulogize my cousin. When my aunt Trudy had approached me for the ask I had known was coming, her voice was raw from sobbing.

"I'll be happy to do it. No problem," I said, hiding my

exhaustion. I wanted to offer comfort to our family; I wanted to find in this tragedy some wisdom that would be useful for the community. But another part of me just wanted to be alone. With the funeral just ten hours away, I faced a blank page. Desperate for inspiration, I played J. Cole's "Can I Live."

More blacks singing more blues,
More niggas pouring more brews,
Poor dude he was young like twenty-one,
straight up out of that city that I'm from . . .

I said a prayer and began to write.

The atmosphere in the church was heavy. It was an all-too-familiar scene in Stockton, the mothers and aunts and grandmothers left to mourn the fragility of the lives of their Black sons. The youth choir that Donnell had been a part of started with the song "Love" by Kirk Franklin. The officiant was our uncle Kevin and he told us how he never thought when he accepted the call to minister, that he would be officiating the funeral of his twenty-year-old nephew.

"Next up, we will have a poem from Donnell's cousin Michael Tubbs, who came all the way from the White House and is at Stanford."

With a deep breath, I walked slowly to the podium, my knees shaking. Trudy had made a request that we didn't wear all black to the funeral, so I had paired a deep blue shirt with my straight-from-the-White-House black suit. I looked down at Donnell's coffin and read the words I'd written.

My Savior lives, and so will I
My Cousin lives, and so I will try
To move past the anger and the rage
To deal with the pain
To see better days
And LIVE.
I gotta laugh, cuz they tried their best
They didn't see the devil proof vest
The substance of things hoped for and evidence of
*   things not seen*
The strength that lies in my family
Despite the lies, still we rise
Despite the wounds, still we rise
Despite the shock, we will rise
Although we cry, we will rise.
As dawn breaks forth and creation sings . . . it's a
*   testimony to the fact that you, Donnell James II*
*   and we have the victory.*
You know after all the Scripture was Right,
Weeping
May endure for a night
But joy
comes in
the morning
Light.

Finished, shaken, I looked out over those who were gathered. I tried to see beyond my fears, beyond my grief and the grief of those present, some sign of a brighter future.

8

REJECTION AND REDIRECTION

At the start of my senior year at Stanford, an execution took place on the opposite side of the country. It shocked the world. Well over half a million signatures had been collected for the petition for clemency, and many organizations and prominent individuals—Amnesty International, Archbishop Desmond Tutu, Pope Benedict XVI, Harry Belafonte, Jesse Jackson, Congressman John Lewis, and the European Parliament, among others—spoke out, requesting the sentence be halted and calling for a new trial. Their pleas fell on deaf ears. The state of Georgia executed Troy Davis via lethal injection on September 21, 2011.

Back in 1989, twenty-one-year-old Troy Davis had found himself in the parking lot of a Burger King in Savannah, Georgia, with a friend, after a pool party. They were there as an argument broke out between a homeless man and a man named Sylvester Coles, owner of a .38 caliber pistol, the weapon that was used to beat the homeless man. An off-duty police officer named Mark McPhail was working as a security guard at the Burger King, and when he tried to intervene and stop the

115

assault, he was shot twice and killed. The weapon was never located.

Sylvester Coles told the police that Troy Davis had assaulted the homeless man, and that he had seen Davis with a .38. (He failed to tell the police he was the owner of a .38 himself, or that he had had the weapon with him on the night of the shooting.) Despite the lack of the murder weapon and any forensic or DNA evidence, testimony from witnesses led to Davis's 1991 conviction, a death verdict. Seven of the nine main witnesses whose testimony led to his conviction later recanted. Many of those who retracted their evidence said that they had been cajoled by police into testifying against Davis. Some said they had been threatened with being put on trial themselves if they did not cooperate. Over time, nine people came forward with evidence to implicate Coles. Yet higher courts repeatedly refused to grant Davis a retrial.

To make matters more tragic, Davis had been scheduled for execution three times before September 2011. In 2008 he had been given a stay just ninety minutes before he was set to die. Mental health experts call these multiple experiences with imminent death "tantamount to torture."

As senior year began, back on campus after my time abroad and in D.C., I was selected by peers to be NAACP president. Troy Davis and the death penalty became the focus of our advocacy efforts, and I soon called a meeting with the Black Student Union to organize an event in Davis's name. I ran the meeting in what had become my customary outcome-focused way—blazing through the agenda, lining up speakers, assigning responsibilities—when the president of the Black Student Union, a sophomore named Anna Malaika Nti-Asare, interrupted me.

"Wait. You're missing the point," she said.

Irritated, I responded with: "What are you talking about?"

"This is not just an event. We're talking about a man's life. He was innocent. This was a person's *life*."

She spoke with such passion that she began to cry.

I was speechless. I functioned by keeping my feelings out of the way, like my mom had taught me. I got things done. Too much emotion was a liability, as far as I was concerned.

But the depth of her empathy, how much she cared, transformed the atmosphere around us. Everyone felt it. I suddenly felt that in protesting Troy's death, I had also set aside a bit of my humanity—the ability to feel the hurt in real time. I leaned over to Cameron and whispered: "I'm going to marry that woman."

"What are you talking about??"

"I'm telling you, she's going to be my wife."

Every year in college had been punctuated, for me, with the murder of Black men. Before Troy Davis, there was Oscar Grant; before Donnell, there were the untimely deaths of other young people in Stockton. During my sophomore year, a year before my cousin's murder, I'd been alarmed by a rash of murder victims all fitting the same description—young, male, minority, all from the part of the city I was raised in— and had called childhood friends studying at the University of the Pacific (UOP) to find out what was going on.

UOP is a top-100 college located in Stockton, and although the majority of students aren't from Stockton, every year a few from our large urban school districts are admitted. The conversations with my friends there turned into a series of brainstorming sessions.

"How did we make it out? What makes us different?"

Those were the two questions that fueled our work. At least one answer was self-evident.

"Education. Right? Ite. Let's open up the UOP campus this summer and show students that there is a better way." I had no previous relationship with the university nor with their staff, but one of my friends, Ty-Licia Hooker, was a student leader and we just knew we would be able to get to a yes, because we were doing the right thing for the right reasons.

The university agreed, and we sprang into action to create the Summer Success and Leadership Academy, targeting students who were considered at-risk. We hoped that we could empower these youth through exposing them to positive role models who looked like them, and through the experience of just being on a university campus. Plus, it would give them something to do at a time when the city's budget cuts meant community centers and libraries had minimal hours (if they were not closed), and sports and arts programs were being cut.

I roped in some students from Stanford, too, and together we created a day-long workshop called "Upset the Setup." The workshop was built upon what had become my worldview: that yes, statistically some groups and some people are set up to fail, but the setup is not destiny. That agency matters and is, in fact, the only thing that will rectify unjust structures. Our goal was to empower these students to Upset the Setup in their lives and the lives of those around them. To believe that they weren't victims, but rather "the masters of their fate and the captains of their souls."

The next summer, before leaving for the White House and knowing the impact that relatable motivational speakers could have, I offered a "Back to School Tour" at two local high schools. I planned to speak about my life thus far, about the perils and promise of coming from Stockton. I had expected to find maybe one hundred of the most difficult students assembled for the event. I was taken aback when I arrived to find the gym crammed with some two thousand students. Looking around, I said a silent prayer. I figured that I had either been set up to fail, or the principal was way too confident in my abilities. If they couldn't get professional teachers to capture the attention of thirty students for one hour, how could they expect a twenty-year-old to capture the attention of the entire school? I'd given my speech at Langston Hughes Academy to five hundred students; two thousand was considerably more.

I took a deep breath and began reciting the poem by Tupac Shakur that has long been a source of inspiration to me: "The Rose That Grew from Concrete."

With Tupac's words to guide me, and with help from Soulja Boy's "Pretty Boy Swag" and Drake's "Best I Ever Had," I kept their attention for the next forty-five minutes. The speech was different from the one I had given at Langston Hughes because now I had seen worlds outside of Stockton. I was living proof that talent is universal, but resources are not. I knew it was hard for these students to see beyond their neighborhoods and their families, but if they could dig deep, there was a whole world waiting for them to explore it. As a high school senior, I had spoken with certainty about the uncertain—my next steps—but couldn't offer much but my abiding faith and examples of how to get to the cusp and reach your goals. Three years later, I was able to speak about what happens when you actually "make it" and how the choices made in high school could impact the next forty years of their lives. I also shared what being away from Stockton for three years had taught me: that growing up in our city had its advantages. It had given me four monumental, transferable skills: Heart, Soul, Resilience, and Swagger.

Stockton had given my audience the very same, I said.

I ran across the gym, fielding questions. "Can someone from Stockton really make it?" one student asked. "How did you do it with a father in jail?" said another. I hoped that by sharing my story I was liberating them to create their own.

Six weeks after Donnell's funeral I was back in Stockton for Christmas break, trying to make sense of things. Over the past year the city had seen its highest rate of homicides in recent history—mostly young men of color, from neighborhoods like mine. Sara Cazares, trustee of the Stockton Unified School Board, invited me to participate in a community forum on violence. I had met her that fall as she dropped her son off for his freshman year at Stanford.

At the meeting I sat with activists and local leaders in a circle of stiff, brown aluminum chairs at the center of a basketball court, brainstorming what we could do to stem the tide of violence. The gym was bare, the colors were faded, and many of us were weary. Father Dean of St. Mary's Church, who had eulogized countless young men with his soft voice and mild stutter, was there. I was impressed with how Trustee Cazares injected life into the meeting by suggesting we adopt the Homeboy Industries model. Created by Father Gregory Boyle in Los Angeles at the end of the 1980s, Homeboy offered substance abuse treatment, tattoo removal, and job training to former gang members.

I offered to do research and anything else to keep the ball

rolling remotely, but I didn't believe I had the time to get too involved. In two weeks, I'd be headed back to Stanford for my final year, and after that, who knew?

I had started my senior year with a clear idea of what I wanted to do after graduation. I was going to be a Rhodes Scholar, which, according to everyone around me, was a smart next step. The selection was in November, so if that didn't work out I had time to consider other things, like going back to the White House or working for a mentor, Marian Wright Edelman, at a D.C. nonprofit called the Children's Defense Fund. I looked forward to seeing where my four years of Stanford would land me.

The Rhodes Scholarship is incredibly competitive, but my advisors assured me that I had the right profile and a stronger chance than most at winning it. Accordingly, I spent countless hours poring over essays, trying to add up my college experiences into a sense of direction. I wrote about my desire to be a part of the policy conversation, reforming laws that had devastated my community, such as redlining and the acts passed during the war on drugs. When I was announced as a Rhodes finalist, it felt like the stars had aligned. The scholarship would set me up with the education and résumé to work wherever I decided I could make the most change. The final round interview was tough, focused not so much on me as on education policy questions, on which I was still no expert. I felt less confident walking out than going in, but I held out hope.

When the Rhodes winners were announced later that afternoon, I wasn't one of them.

Feelings of inadequacy immediately surfaced. I questioned whether I was on the right path at all. Objectively, I knew the Rhodes wasn't a sure thing for anyone, but it had aligned with what I thought I was meant to do. I was unnerved. In the days and weeks after the rejection, I dug deep into why I had wanted the Rhodes in the first place.

As the meeting with Stockton's leaders drew to a close, I went over to Trustee Cazares to thank her for the invitation. She asked me how things were at Stanford and what I was planning to do after I graduated.

"To be honest, man, no idea," I responded. "Taking time over this winter break to really sit down and figure that out."

"Well, how many more people have to die before you feel ready to come back?"

"I hear you," I muttered.

Growing up, getting out was the name of the game. Success was defined as leaving Stockton and not looking back. The previous three years had provided a global perspective and a sense of unlimited possibilities. At the same time, the murder of Donnell and the Rhodes rejection seemingly pointed to a path that led me back home after graduation.

As Christmas break stretched on, I thought about my vow to the kids of Langston Hughes three years earlier: to find a way back to Stockton. And I thought about the poem I'd written to Donnell and read the next day through tears. Lines came back to me:

> *Figuring out how to change tragedy to triumph*
> *And finding escape from the abyss*
> *But if I know nothing I know this*
> *All Things are Working Together*
> *For my Good,*
> *For my Hood.*

I entertained other thoughts, but I couldn't bring myself to complete applications or attend interviews. On paper, consulting firms and fellowships seemed like safe and logical next steps, but they didn't feel right. They didn't feel in alignment with where my heart was: home. Home, with the circle of chairs in the faded gymnasium, with inspiring leaders, ordinary people trying to create a better future in the hood.

"You're going to do what?!"

I looked away.

"Michael, look at me. You don't owe anyone anything. And you've been helping! Hell, you do more than most people here! This is what you went to Stanford for?! If anyone else had the chance to make it out like you did, they would."

"Mom, I'm just thinking about it, it's an option. I'll explore it and we'll see."

"Uh-huh," she said, eyeing me with a mixture of suspicion and pride. Her mother's intuition was in high gear, and she tried to convince me during the rest of Christmas break that Stockton's issues weren't going anywhere and weren't worth the effort of trying to solve them.

Watching the local news only strengthened my resolve. In an interview, the mayor was asked for a status update on the city's "Marshall Plan" to address intergenerational crime, which she had announced with fanfare during her State of the City address earlier in the year. Now she replied that she had no idea what the reporter was referencing. It touched a nerve in me. Violence and poverty were the most important issues of the city, yet the mayor's lack of urgency reflected a disconnect between her own reality and the reality of most people living in Stockton.

My time at the White House had illustrated to me that local

elected officials did not have magic wands, but they did have the power to raise morale and to serve as catalysts for change, even if incremental. I saw, now, that the policy-making table in Stockton was where solutions could scale, where my Stanford education could be put to use immediately. No one with my experiences and perspective had been in the room where it happens in my hometown. The situation was dire, and my solution felt a bit scary, but my decision was made.

Switching off the TV, I called my best friend, Cameron.

"I've decided to run for city council."

A month after the meeting during which we organized the protest of Troy Davis's execution, I asked Anna Malaika Nti-Asare out for dinner. I took her to my favorite restaurant, an Ethiopian place called Zeni in San Jose. It's the best Ethiopian restaurant in the state, possibly the nation. I was fifteen minutes late picking her up, since I had stopped to wash my car, trying to make everything as presentable as possible. Little did I know she was a very punctual person and considered lateness a form of disrespect.

I got lost driving to the restaurant, too, which was crazy, since I went there all the time. I hoped Anna didn't notice how nervous I was. (She absolutely did.) I turned on some music: J. Cole's "In the Morning" played, *Baby, you summertime fine . . .*

Finally, we got to the restaurant. In the front section they have tables and chairs, and in the back you're seated in traditional Ethiopian manner, on leather cushions at low tables made of woven straw. We sat in the traditional section. A live band tucked in a wall alcove played live Ethiopian music. I managed to make her laugh. It seemed to be going well.

I asked Anna where she was from, what her family was like,

and what she cared about. One thing we had in common, I learned, was our ambivalence about attending Stanford before we arrived. Anna had thought she'd wind up at a smaller liberal arts school. Stanford was the only large school she had visited. As the daughter of two international lawyers, her mother from Washington state, of Swedish descent, and her father from Accra, Ghana, she'd lived in a dozen countries by the time she was twelve years old. Her racial identity wasn't salient to her growing up, having been exposed to so many places abroad with her white mother and always being one of the few Black children in her community. When she got placed in the Ujaama dorm, she didn't think she would be able to relate. But by the end of her first day, Anna realized that her unique experience of Blackness didn't mean she didn't belong in the Black community.

I found out that we had interacted before planning the protest for Troy Davis. She reminded me that the year before, during her freshman year, when Jan flew me back to campus from D.C. to speak at a homecoming event, she came up to compliment me on my speech. She said that I responded with a "Thank you. You're my favorite freshman." I still have no recollection of that first encounter. Sheepishly, I said that I was probably jet-lagged.

Anna was impressive. At the end of her freshman year, she was selected co-president of the Black Student Union, a position unheard of for a sophomore. She wasn't intimidated by me even though I was two years older. She was worldly, that much was clear, and I felt grateful that I had traveled to at least a couple places outside the United States before meeting her.

She was so engrossed in our conversation at Zeni, meanwhile, that she forgot to wash her hands—and you eat Ethiopian food with your hands. As awed as I was by her, I had to

interrupt the conversation: "We should go wash our hands."
This oversight was not a sign of things to come. Anna is a neat
freak, and I'm pretty messy.

Part of Anna's intrigue, besides her undeniable beauty, ra-
diant smile, and kind heart, was just how different our backgrounds were. Whereas Stockton was synonymous with home
for me, for Anna the concept of home wasn't tied to a place at
all. She'd grown up in Estonia, Azerbaijan, Dubai, Monterrey,
Mexico, Wyoming, boarding school in Indiana, and elsewhere.
For her, home was more about relationships than place.

On the way back to campus I asked what kind of music she
listened to. She didn't know who J. Cole was, which shocked
me, as he was the most played artist on my iTunes. She clearly
didn't have all the intricacies of American Black culture down.
I made it my mission to fill in the gaps and started her with
a steady diet of Black movies, like *Set It Off*, *Paid in Full*, *Juice*,
and *Waiting to Exhale*.

But she loved Tupac. "You don't know Cole, but you love
Pac?" I asked. "Yeah, when I was traveling, Tupac gave me a
window to understanding what it meant to be Black, even
though I wasn't in America." I was a little doubtful that she
knew what she was talking about. But then I put on "Keep
Ya Head Up" and she started rapping. She knew every word
and even rapped with a little swag. My fondness grew.

I mentioned that I hadn't gotten the Rhodes Scholarship.

"So what are you going to do after graduation?" Anna
asked me.

"I'm thinking about running for city council in my hometown," I told her, keeping it sounding casual.

"Cool," she replied.

She didn't realize I was dead serious.

9

SPRINT

Here goes nothing," I said to myself as I took a deep breath and knocked on my first door. Although outwardly calm, I was nervous. I didn't want to feel like an imposition, nor did I want to stare rejection in the face. Figurative closed doors were hard enough to deal with; literal doors slammed in your face, a whole 'nother story! *What if I'm too young? What if they think this is a joke?* I thought.

The door opened to reveal an African American man around forty.

"Hello, sir, my name is Michael Tubbs and I am running for city council in this area."

"Word?"

"Yes, sir! I'm from here, was able to go to Stanford, interned at Google and the White House, and now want to come home and help our city reach its full potential."

"Really? Stanford?! From here . . . Babe, come here! You gotta look at this young man running for Congress!"

His wife came out and looked me up and down. "You running for Congress?"

"No, ma'am. Stockton City Council. I'm interested in hearing more about your ideas on how to improve the city and this neighborhood."

The man—his name was Eric—seemed excited that I asked his opinion. He pointed up: "You see this streetlight? It's been out for a year or so now. It gets real dark at night, unsafe. I don't let my daughter go outside."

As I furiously took notes, he shared how he lived in Stockton only half the year, as the other half of the year he was forced to leave his wife and daughter to go to Alaska for work.

"There's no work for you here?"

"Nah, not that pays a decent wage and I'm qualified for." He paused, looked at me thoughtfully, and continued: "I want better for my daughter. She's smart. Good at music too. I want her to be like you: go to school, have options. Opportunities. Man, it's so good to see a positive, young Black man trying to make a change. You have our support."

Almost an hour had passed and I had only knocked on one door. Before I could leave, Eric took me around to everyone out on the street, introducing me: "He's not afraid to come to talk to us!"

Eric lived in Conway. Conway Homes is a Housing Authority development in South Stockton, one of the neighborhoods considered "the projects." Built after World War II and more or less unchanged since, it's one of those places people are happy to escape from, to which you only go because either you live there or you have family there. Conway's reputation was that it was crime- and drug-ridden, filled with lazy, unemployed people who were part of the city's deficits, as opposed to assets. This view was pervasive in more affluent and whiter parts of the city, but was also internalized by many of the communities adjacent and surrounding the development. About ten minutes away from where I grew up, Conway served as my papa's (my mother's father) childhood home, where his family and many others like his settled after migrating from the South. Meant as a starting place before a transition to non-government-supported housing, some of his brothers and their children still lived there, sixty-plus years after the family arrived.

Oftentimes, poverty in Stockton is a family heirloom.

Despite the challenges, there was a vibrant community in Conway, with fierce resident council advocates who petitioned the Housing Authority Commission, parents who wanted nothing more than opportunity for their children, and periodic block parties where the full diversity of the community—Black, Southeast Asian, Mexican, and white—was on full display.

Across the street from Eric's house was the Van Buskirk Community Center. I had spent many hours there playing in recreational ball leagues. I didn't get much time to hang out in the neighborhood before or after our games, but those rec league battles were fierce. I associated life lessons with that court, like my mother's admonishment to "not let them see you cry" after a loss, or Coach Paul's advice that "Defense wins championships. You gotta hustle." As a positive space for children, Van Buskirk was Conway's community nucleus. Looking across the street, I wondered if I should hold my campaign kickoff in its gym. The space was huge, and I reckoned it was as nostalgic for others as it was for me.

As I hugged him good-bye, Eric said: "We need you to be congressman." I gently corrected him, reminding him I was running for city council. He looked at me and said, "Oh yeah. We can start there. But I like saying Congressman Tubbs."

I spoke to local political consultants about my idea to start the campaign at Van Buskirk and was met with a mix of condescension and confusion. They asked why I would want to hold an event in one of the most economically depressed parts of the city, and countered with somewhere more traditional, like city hall or an upscale restaurant in North Stockton to appeal to a wider base. Besides, I was told, the gym was too big. It would feel empty and I'd feel like I had no support.

I doubled down on the idea. I was running precisely because I believed those in power didn't view places like Van Buskirk as important, nor did they view those who lived around places like Van Buskirk as important. I told my team that our campaign was going to be about centering the "least of these," a focus that came from the Scripture in Matthew when Jesus said, *When I was hungry did you feed me? When I was naked did you clothe me? When I was imprisoned did you visit me? As you do to the least of these, you do unto me.*

Stockton's six part-time councilmembers, along with the full-time mayor, had the responsibility of setting the priorities of a city of over three hundred thousand. I was running because I knew there were people whose priorities weren't being taken into account. So, from the beginning, I was going to talk to people most politicians don't talk to, and I believed that was how we were going to win.

After every voter canvass we spent an hour as a team, tracking volunteer counts and going over budgets. We used my favorite organizing tool, a white board and marker, courtesy of the meeting rooms at UOP. Cameron was there, having sacrificed senior year shenanigans to troubleshoot and do design work for me, as was my friend Ty-Licia Hooker, with whom I had worked on the Summer Success and Leadership Academy. The rest of my initial team consisted of folks who weren't from the donor class nor from political backgrounds, but were the fabric of Stockton, the Stockton so routinely left out of "the room where it happens." There was my debate coach in high school, Tama Brisbane; Trustee Sara Cazares, the school board member; and, of course, the three titans: my mom, my aunt Tasha, and my grandmother. Our campaign headquarters was, at least for now, my mom's house. "Just make sure you transfer thirty dollars into my account so people can keep their shoes on in the house and I can get the carpet shampooed after," my mom said in advance of our first meeting.

It was at that first gathering, just after New Year's 2012, that we decided on the theme of my campaign. Cameron, who had quietly taken notes throughout, summarized: "What I'm hearing is that Stockton is in need of a reinvention."

"Reinvent Stockton it is!" was my reply.

After a month of knocking on every door in the Conway community, voter and nonvoter alike, I grew accustomed to the exclamation: "You are the first person to ever knock on my door and ask me directly for my vote!" This was generally followed with infuriating stories of neglect and marginalization.

Many folks were also puzzled, asking me the question that my mom did: "Why on earth did you choose to come back?"

Several of my mentors at Stanford had also protested my decision. Stockton had more homicides per capita than Chicago and was looking like it would become the largest city in American history to declare bankruptcy. My opponent for the District 6 city council seat, Dale Fritchen, was a formidable one, as he was an incumbent with over a decade of local government experience and was chair of the San Joaquin

County Republican Party. Despite its diversity, Stockton was not a overwhelmingly Democratic city but had a sizable number of Republican and Decline to State voters.

"Are you sure this is the opportune time for you?" "There's no win here." "Why don't you wait for all the hard stuff to figure itself out and then run for office in a decade or so? The issues in Stockton aren't going anywhere." These were the sentiments shared by Stanford professors who encouraged me to instead apply for law school, or to look into working for them.

Only Jan Barker Alexander was unflinchingly supportive. "What does your mom think?" she asked, and she listened intently as I explained my mom's resistance: the ugliness of politics, her belief that Stockton was a dead end and not much could be done to improve it, her desire for me to enjoy life, to make money, to help support her. Then Jan smiled.

"I think you should do it. It'll be the challenge of a lifetime, but all your time at Stanford seems to have been pointing to this moment."

Then: "How can I help?" She sprang to action, emailing her Stanford network to marshal support for my nascent campaign.

Many constituents two and three times my age exclaimed that they hoped their children or grandchildren would end up like me. While political consultants were adamant that I de-emphasize my youth, at Conway I learned that voters were genuinely impressed that a twenty-one-year-old would want to be a part of the political process.

"We need that young blood, them fresh ideas. Them old people are stuck in their ways and don't care!"

So I went ahead and wore my Jordan 3s as opposed to

my dress shoes for walking around and knocking on doors. Every time my mom or aunt reminded me that they never saw a politician wear kicks, I would gently remind them that I was twenty-one, my Jordans were fresh, and I wasn't yet a politician—I was an aspiring one!

On Spring Street, a street so synonymous with crime that I was forbidden to go there as a child, most of the doors I knocked on went unopened, although I could hear the volume of the television turned down and the yapping of Chihuahuas. At the last door on the street, Ms. Ortiz opened her door after a delay. She was older, but that wasn't why it took a while for her to appear: it was the number of locks on her door, more than I'd ever seen. She had barricaded herself inside.

Ms. Ortiz eyed me warily as I introduced myself and my aims. She told me how she routinely slept on the floor with her two young children, as gunshots were pervasive. The house next door—she gestured to it and I said I'd noticed the number of cars coming and going—was a drug house.

I noticed her son peering through the window repeatedly. "Is he okay?" I asked. She replied, "Sure, he just has never seen me outside on the porch talking to anyone." She told me how he had developed asthma because of the pervasive gun smoke and the other environmental toxins in the neighborhood coupled with the overall poor air quality and lack of trees, and how he had also developed stomach ulcers from anxiety. "He does good in school though. He's on honor roll."

Ms. Ortiz thanked me for our conversation, told me I had her full support, that she hoped her children turned out like me, and gave me a hug. As I left, I assured her that I would not forget her, or the issues in her community. The story of her son stuck with me, and not because of the ulcers, or sleeping on the floor. It was because despite those challenges, the tough neighborhood he was growing up in and his health challenges and anxieties, he had made the honor roll. These were difficult circumstances. In this family's story I saw the same drive and determination that had enabled me to get to Stanford. It remained a reminder of the stakes of the election and why I had decided to come back to Stockton in the first place. Yes, it was beautiful to see another rose grow from concrete, but it also was a stark reminder that roses deserved better soil in the first place.

I had grown up in the council district I sought to represent, but going door to door and immersing myself in the community provided me with a reintroduction to my hometown. In my conversations, I heard experiences about the labor market that were similar to my mother's, stories of incarceration that were similar to my father's, and experiences with tragedy and loss that were similar to my family's experience with Donnell. I heard a belief that government may work for and care about some people, but not people like "us," and that, although they wished me luck, they didn't see my victory as likely. Armed with these insights from a community most "experts" assumed didn't care about politics at all, I was ready to have my campaign kickoff on February 20, 2012.

The venue would indeed be the gymnasium of the Van Buskirk Community Center. Nicholas Hatten, the local Democratic Party chair whom I was trying to convince to be my campaign manager, was so concerned that the event would be underattended and the cavernous space would look ridiculous with only the few dozen he expected might attend, that he held off joining the campaign until after the kickoff.

"Nicholas, trust me. I'm from here. People know me. People will come." He wasn't convinced by my bravado, having had much more experience than I predicting the customary turnout for a first-time candidate.

Aunt Tasha served as treasurer for the campaign, while my mom and Nana were whips, going through their contacts to ensure a good turnout. Nana phone banked all of her church friends and former co-workers, laughing while saying, "Yeah, Mike decided to come back! He wants to do good and needs your support." My mom and aunt convinced Cynthia Jackson, their hairdresser, to jump on board, and between the three of them reached out to all of her clients, especially the well-to-do ones. Cameron led operations at Stanford, where he and another close friend, Karl, organized phone banks and set up a car pool for Stanford students to, as they pitched it, "Come down to Stockton and be a part of something special." My cousin Scharlyce; little brother, Dre; and godbrother Isaiah led the volunteer efforts. Along with my mother and Nana, they were in charge of serving the food, which Isaiah's mom and dad catered as part of their new catering business. I decided to keep the order simple for them with hot dogs and hamburgers.

I had never attended a campaign kickoff and didn't bother to ask those that had what they were like. From what I had gathered from skeptical consultants, I surmised that they were boring and dry. I wanted to do something fun, that people would remember: spoken word, a live band playing "A Change Is Gonna Come," and a vision board of brown butcher paper hung around the gym where people could express their hopes and dreams for Stockton.

The day came. I put on my black suit. My only suit. Sara

Cazares bought me a red tie. "This is the ultimate power tie," she said. When Cameron arrived, he examined me critically, and after a moment, took off his own watch and gave it to me to wear. "You got to have a nice watch, bro. It'll make you look presidential."

A half hour before the start time, there were barely any cars in the Van Buskirk parking lot. The band was set up, the tarp was on the floor, the food was ready, but the gym suddenly felt too massive. I told Scharlyce and Dre to only pull out half the bleachers so the space would look more full. I tried to project calm, but was consumed with anxiety. I went outside the back of the gym to practice my speech, which turned into many minutes of pacing back and forth and praying and thinking, *What if everyone was right? What if we were too ambitious? What if people don't believe that this is possible?*

"Bro, it's 11:00 A.M."

"I don't care what time it is, Cameron, are people here?"

"Yeah, man! People rolled out for you!"

I walked into the gym and found a crowd of more than 150 people making their way to the bleachers. There were young people who had been a part of the Summer Success and Leadership Academy, with their families. There were Stanford classmates whom I led in the Phoenix Scholars and the NAACP. There were recreation league basketball coaches, pastors, city planning commissioners, former councilmembers, and a handful of Conway residents we had talked to over the past month. Some of those in attendance we had reached out to individually, but many came because they heard about the event in the *Record* or by word of mouth.

Walking inside, I looked at Cameron and said, "This looks like a winning coalition."

Kicking off the event was Francisco Gaio, one of my favorite students from the Summer Success and Leadership Academy and the student body president at my alma mater, Franklin High. He was nattily attired in a suit, and shared the pressure he felt as president of Franklin High School to live up to what I had done while I was president. He talked about the impact of SSLA and the Phoenix Scholars on his development and said that I had illustrated to him that everyone could become a superhero through service. His remarks caught me off guard, and I felt my emotions rise. Ellen Powell, a representative for the local assembly member, explained to the crowd why she was supporting a twenty-one-year-old political novice for office and how she believed in my leadership and ability to move the city forward. She closed out the introductions revival-style, hyping the crowd by imploring them to be proud of the young man they had collectively raised as a village, a young man who had decided to come back and serve. She reminded us that we were not just gathered for a campaign, but to launch opportunity and a vision for Stockton. She said that I represented what happens when Nana's prayers, Mom's love, and the village's support conspire to provide opportunity for a young person. She concluded with a call and response, whipping the crowd into thundering excitement: "Vote for Tubbs!"

I hadn't written out my speech, and as I took the floor I was a ball of adrenaline. I just went for it, retelling the assembled crowd a story with which all of them were almost certainly familiar, the story of a young, inexperienced shepherd boy who went up against the giant that was threatening his community. The shepherd boy had appealed to the king for help, to no avail, and then decided that if the people with the titles wouldn't do it, if the experts wouldn't do it, and if the generals wouldn't do it, then he would have to do it. The king offered the shepherd boy his tools of war, but the shepherd boy declined them, and told the king that those were the tools that had created the problem and that he would be using other tools. He collected five smooth stones for his slingshot.

"You all know the end of this story," I told the crowd, who cheered and applauded until the whole gym vibrated.

"I've been fighting giants my whole life," I said. "The media and the experts who told me that, growing up as I did, I had two options: prison or death. The teachers who told me I'd never get into Stanford, and once I got in, that I would fail. I kept defeating the giants."

In Stockton, I told them, we had many giants to slay. There was crime. One-third of the fifty-three homicides that happened in Stockton in the previous year had taken place in this district, District 6. There was poverty. Thirty-five percent of the residents in District 6 were living in poverty. There was a school district that was a dead end for too many students. But there were giants beyond these issues, too: incompetent leadership and a political establishment that had no familiarity with the issues it made decisions about and that believed that big money was the only way to win a political campaign.

What were the five stones of this shepherd boy? Faith. Education. Experience. The Obama White House. And, finally, the Community: everyone who was listening and believing, and who would come to listen and believe in the coming months.

The kickoff felt like a celebration. But it was only February, and the journey had only just begun.

* * *

In the excitement of my campaign announcement and candidacy, many well-meaning people signed my Declaration of Candidacy form, ignoring the provision that they had to be registered voters of my district. The form only required ten signatures, but I made sure that we had thirty of them to be safe. I also thought I had made sure to share with everyone that they had to be a registered voter in District 6 to sign.

On the day before I needed sufficient signatures to qualify for the ballot, the city clerk called me. "If you don't submit valid signatures by tomorrow morning you will be ineligible to run for office."

"Are you shitting me?" was Nicholas Hatten's response to the news. "Dude, how are we going to get those signatures?"

I called upon God. More specifically, I texted one of the more civically minded pastors in my district, Pastor Trena Turner. She invited me to come to her church for Bible study that very evening. At the conclusion of the service, she gave me a couple of minutes to address the congregation and reminded them that they had to live in District 6 in order to sign my form. By the time I left her congregation, I had more than enough valid signatures.

To my profuse thanks, Pastor Trena responded, "God works in mysterious ways, Mr. Tubbs. Remember that."

Over the next weeks I learned that a campaign entailed much more than a kickoff. Thankfully, Nicholas Hatten was an asset from the jump, with an invaluable combination of street smarts, understanding of people, relationships, and grit. Half Black and half Latino, he had founded and ran the first Pride Center in San Joaquin County with tenacity and vision. And, as promised, he had come on board as my campaign manager despite his initial reservations, which included not just my lack of experience, but also my ties to the Black church. He understandably feared that parishioners might object to a gay man running my campaign. I had told him not to worry, that I'd handle that, and if we had to educate some people about homophobia along the way, it would be a win-win.

We disagreed about some fine points of my strategy thus far. "Michael, you are a candidate, not an activist! Time is your greatest resource. You can't go knock on every single door in every single neighborhood and talk to every single person. Yeah, everyone matters and you govern for everyone, but the sad reality is that everyone doesn't vote! We need to micro-target and use walk lists to ensure that we are prioritizing and talking to the people who we know for sure vote, as they have voted in the past."

"Nick, I don't disagree. How do I do that? Where do I get walk lists from? I thought we just literally knocked on doors and talked to people."

His exasperation at my naïveté regularly dissolved into benign chuckles. He explained the pivot in strategy to the team—Cameron, Sara, my moms, my youth volunteers—and met no objections. Trying to talk to everyone, unbeknownst to me, was exhausting my campaign team, and we had just started.

Given that I was simultaneously in my final semester at Stanford, going for not just my bachelor's in Comparative Studies in Race and Ethnicity, but also my master's degree in education, Nicholas's point about time being my greatest resource could not have been more true. I was not only completing the necessary twenty-three units for those degrees and writing my honor's thesis, I was still serving as Stanford

NAACP's president and as executive director of the Phoenix Scholars as well. I was haunted with visions of my opponent running negative ads of me saying that I was a college drop-out or unable to graduate, given that one of the most compelling parts of my campaign narrative was that I was going to be a Stanford graduate.

Nick was also adamant about the need to do "call time," which to this day remains one of my least favorite activities.

"Michael, I'm going to hand you this phone and list of all the people you need to contact and ask them to give you money."

Eyes rolling, I retorted, "I don't like asking people with no money for money."

If Nicholas had his way, I would do call time for two hours every day. "Our congressman does that!" he would remind me. But I hated it. He tried to force me to call everyone in my phone contacts list and ask for donations, ranging from five to five hundred dollars, but we reached a compromise by which I texted my contacts instead. In the end I only texted those who I believed had the disposable income to give. Nicholas also gave me a list of local Democratic donors to ask for money. It felt fake and transactional to call people I had never met before out the blue and ask for money, so I would ask them to coffee or lunch first, and then do a follow-up call for dollars. That elongated the fundraising time, and more than once I heard some version of "Mr. Tubbs, I'll donate. We don't have to get lunch. Your time is important."

Call time was difficult for me, in part, because of the vulnerability it required. I had been taught to be independent, to ask for help sparingly. Donor calls seemingly required the inverse of that.

Accordingly, my fundraising numbers were low. As we

entered the month of March, we had only raised ten thousand dollars, less than a third of the thirty-six thousand dollars my opponent, Dale Fritchen, had in his war chest.

The grind of the campaign began to take its toll. It was exhausting to have to say good-bye to Anna at 5:00 A.M. after reaching her room—exhausted—at midnight the night before, so that I could drive the two hours back home to Stockton. We had only just started dating in earnest, and being too worn out to do anything but sleep during our precious hours together was not a great start to what I hoped would be a serious relationship.

Because I was campaigning full-time, I also had to quit my student jobs, and my checking account constantly flirted with being in overdraft. Every trip to the gas station was an exercise in miracles; I had to pass the offering hat around to my family and occasionally Cameron to cover the gas and the five-dollar toll to ensure I could get back and forth from Stockton to Palo Alto. I dreaded asking my mother or my aunt for twenty or thirty dollars that I knew they didn't have, but I also knew that they always had my back. Before field trips in elementary school, my mom would take the "penny box," a shoe box that served as our piggy bank, to Coinstar to convert the coins to cash so I would have at least twenty dollars' spending money. Both my mom and Tasha would work overtime and weekends beginning in the summer, every year, to ensure that we had enough gifts under the Christmas tree. I had planned to not have to keep asking them to sacrifice for me by the time I was ready to graduate college.

I was expected to be in a suit at every public appearance. I only had one suit and one pair of dress shoes. Resources being what they were, going from one suit to two had been all I could manage, and I had to become more mindful while eating so as not to stain them. Sara Cazares must have noticed this, as every time I met with her, she greeted me with an expensive tie that she just had happened to pick up and thought would look good on me.

It also proved difficult to sustain the enthusiasm of volunteers, who had their own lives to live. Frustration reached an apex when I arrived for a weekly precinct walk and not a single person showed up—not my family, not my close friends, not even Nicholas, although, as my campaign manager, he was the only paid person on staff! My aunt eventually arrived to drop off precinct lists and walk sheets, but soon left.

For the first time in the campaign, I felt utterly alone. I collapsed on the couch. A wave of self-pity crested: I felt the futility of my efforts, the sacrifices of time with Anna and the fun of senior year. *Maybe I'm not the one to help Reinvent Stockton. Maybe I was hearing my ego and not my calling. Maybe a twenty-one-year-old running for city council is as crazy as it sounds*, I thought.

Two weeks earlier, there had been a bright spot when Jan Barker Alexander invited me to an event at the Stanford Faculty Club, the venue where I had met Valerie Jarrett a few years prior. Despite everything I had going on, I accepted the invite, knowing it would feature something out of the ordinary. And, at a minimum, a luxurious meal.

At Jan's urging, I overcame my relaxed attitude to punctuality and arrived ten minutes early, just in time to see the special guests arrive: Oprah Winfrey, together with two students from her leadership academy in South Africa. I knew that Oprah was a big deal, but my moms didn't watch her show every single day. I knew that she had a larger-than-life personality, but didn't realize that she was about the height of my 5'7" mother. As she entered the faculty club, she brought a regal energy with her. Not that she thought she was better than anyone else, but that she knew exactly who she was and loved herself fully. As we sat down, though, I decided that I would spend my time talking to her students, as it's difficult to impress impressive people and the stated purpose of the luncheon was to give the South African students a sense of Stanford. I spoke earnestly with the young women about life on campus and shared my opinion that the Ujaama dorm had the same community feel as Mizoli's *braai*.

When the server came around, Oprah ordered grilled cheese and tomato soup. (I ordered grilled salmon with fries.) After the meals were served, the Dean led a round of introductions. As it drew to my turn, I thought about whether to mention that I was running for city council. *Nah*, I decided, *that ain't what you're here for.*

When I left out that detail, though, Jan and the dean jumped in to expand on my introduction. My accomplishments were laid out without me having to say them myself.

Like the midday sun, Oprah turned the full force of her attention on me then, asking who was supporting me and how much money I'd raised. The questions came rapid fire and it felt like a campaign strategy session as I shared with Oprah the nitty-gritty details: my vision for Stockton, the stray and guard dogs that were constant companions as I knocked on doors, the lack of support I'd seen from the political establishment in Stockton, the endorsements I had secured, and the ten thousand dollars I had raised thus far.

Having heard me out, she said that she had only supported a couple of campaigns previously—and asked how she could give to mine. A hush fell on the table as everyone took in the magnitude of the moment.

After the luncheon, as we escorted Oprah to her car, she asked to take a photo with me and requested my contact information. She called me Councilman Tubbs. Afterward I sent the picture to Nicholas, who responded simply "HARPO!!!"

Two weeks later, I found myself on the couch feeling utterly alone and defeated. A celebrity meeting, it turned out, could not overcome weeks of mounting financial stress, frustration, and uncertainty. I thought about what a relief it would be, in some ways, to let go. What's the worst that could happen if I never became "Councilman Tubbs"?

Before using my last ten dollars to put gas in the car to head back to Stanford, I had an urge to check the mailbox. In there was an envelope from OWM. I had no idea what OWM was and cursed my luck. *Oh great! A bill I didn't anticipate that I won't be able to pay,* I thought to myself as I put the envelope, unopened, on the table. But before I could reach the door, my curiosity got the best of me and I circled back to the table to open the envelope. In it was a ten-thousand-dollar check from Oprah Winfrey Management.

I cried. I laughed. I shook my head in disbelief. I learned that there will always be provision for purpose-rooted visions. I vowed never to question my decision to return home and to run for office again.

10

VICTORY LAP

June 5, 2012—Primary Election Day—came, and there was no turning back. Anna had surprised me with a watch as a good-luck gift. I still wasn't sure whether our relationship would last the rigors of the campaign and whatever happened once I graduated (fingers crossed), since she had two more years at Stanford. I was touched by the gesture in any case. As I put on my slacks, my freshly pressed dress shirt, and Anna's watch, I said a prayer and took a deep breath. We had done all we could do, and my fate rested in the hands of the voters. My mantra in the weeks leading up to the primaries was one I'd been told as a child: *Work as if it all depends on you and pray as if it all depends on God. With that combination you can't lose.*

My mother's garage was converted into the Get Out the Vote headquarters. We rented tables and chairs from the church, printed out precinct maps and walk lists, and had bananas and water ready for all of the volunteers who would help us make sure those who said they supported me would actually vote in a low-turnout June primary. In triple-digit weather, my volunteers and I made calls, went to check polling places, and even drove folks to the polls. After three hours and only five confirmed voters on my part, my confidence began to flag. As I approached the garage again, however, I saw the volunteers—friends, friends' parents, church mothers, students—laughing as they worked. I marveled at the civic engagement right in front of me. *Whether we win or lose,* I thought, *we did something right.*

At 5:00 P.M., we gathered to watch the election returns. I was uncharacteristically silent. My phone kept lighting up with messages asking, "How did you do?" until I had to put it away. The vote counts were slow, and the butterflies in my stomach churned harder as the minutes passed. A reporter from the *Los Angeles Times* who had been assigned to follow me for the day asked, "What's going on in your mind right now?" I refused to tell her I was nervous that all of our efforts had been in vain, instead forcing a smile that projected the confidence I so desperately wanted.

A collective hush fell and all eyes were glued to the television as the returns for the Stockton City Council race were announced. On the screen flashed: *Stockton City Council District 6, Michael Tubbs 56 percent, Dale Fritchen 44 percent.*

We hadn't just won the primary. We had beaten the incumbent by over ten points to become the only council challenger in the city to emerge on top. We still had the general election in November to win, but this was an essential first step. It showed that I wasn't just a novelty candidate for council seat. I was a serious contender.

Immediately after the primary, my attention swung to completing my coursework. Every day I worked maniacally until five in the morning, wearing my favorite red Stanford hoodie and my green Jordan shorts, taking short naps and subsisting on a diet of cheese sticks, shrimp fried rice, and milkshakes, the staples of Lagunita Dining Late Night, my after–10:00 P.M. campus eatery since my freshman year. As graduation day drew closer, I turned in my eighty-five-page honor's thesis, an evaluation of the impact of the Summer Success and Leadership Academy on participants' subsequent feelings toward school and achievement, and my master's classes' response papers, and hoped for the best. I was able to enjoy the last few days of senior year before preparing the speeches I had been selected to give at Stanford's Black Graduation, a longstanding tradition to celebrate the accomplishments of Black students, and a speech for the ceremony for my undergraduate major, Comparative Studies in Race and Ethnicity.

The night before graduation, at the Senior Dinner on the Quad, a fancy multicourse meal with a lot of wine and dancing, I recounted with friends the most hilarious moments from the past four years. The sun set and I took to the dance floor, just another college kid. Around midnight I felt a vibration in my pocket and checked my email.

> Dear Michael Tubbs,
> I am pleased to inform you that your Spring Quarter 2011–12 application to graduate has been approved for the following degree(s):
> BA in Comparative Studies in Race and Ethnicity with Honors
> MA in Education
> You have satisfied all University and departmental requirements for the degree(s) listed above.

Overwhelmed with emotion, I hugged friends. I grabbed Cameron and exclaimed that our kids wouldn't have to struggle the way I had; they would grow up in a world knowing that people like their parents and uncles and aunts went to Stanford. Evan, my friend from study abroad, and I met on the middle of the dance floor and hugged with the euphoria of a journey ending. I ran looking for a quiet place and called my mom, sobbing.

"Hello, Michael. You okay?"

"Mom, I'm graduating. We really did it. Mom, we're Stanford graduates. Everything was worth it."

"God is so good! So good!" she cried with me before three-waying Aunt Tasha and Nana so they could join in.

I received the Lloyd W. Dinkelspiel Award, the highest honor given to a graduating senior, for "efforts to provide opportunities for the underserved—and to inspire others to do so as well—both on campus and in his hometown of Stockton." This resulted in an invitation for me and my family to a reception with Stanford trustees and the year's commencement speaker, Mayor Cory Booker. I wondered how my mother and aunt would feel in that high-powered room; they didn't seem nervous, but did express surprise that so many "important" people wanted to meet them.

The dignitaries treated my family as VIPs. It brought a smile to my face: only in America could a teenage mother with no college degree hold court with a prominent mayor and the chair of the Stanford University Board of Trustees. When they asked her for parenting tips, she shrugged. "I just did what every parent does or should do."

Black Graduation was the seminal event for the Black

student community, even more so than general commencement. As part of the ceremony, we were allowed to bring two people on stage to bestow on us the traditional *kente* cloth (a patterned stole with roots in the royal ceremonies of the Asante people of West Africa). That wasn't going to be quite enough for me. The day belonged to three women equally, so I directed all of them to stand in line at one end of the stage.

"Mikey, the announcement said only two of us can go on stage, so I'll sit down," said my nana, always one to follow protocol.

"Nana, it's fine, I want you up there with me. We'll be okay."

As my name was called, I hit my dougie and my mom ran across the stage to meet me in a mixture of a dance and hug. She clapped her hands and walked in a circle as the others caught up. Nana seemed embarrassed by all the attention and Tasha just cried as she looked up into the heavens. Our joy was palpable as my three titans bestowed the *kente* cloth upon me, the man they had raised.

Finally, Jan Barker Alexander introduced me before I gave the final remarks.

"Only the third person Oprah has endorsed after Barack Obama and Cory Booker: you can't tell me God ain't good!" she informed the crowd. It felt right that Jan had joined my other three moms onstage, because I considered her my fourth mother, at Stanford.

I took a breath, closed my eyes briefly, and did my best to do justice to the four years of growth and struggle. I began:

> As I welcomed the New Year in 2009, midway through our freshman year, I sat in my dorm room and cried. Oscar Grant had just been murdered in

Oakland, someone who looked just like me, and I began to feel guilty about being a student at Stanford University. This past year, the same feelings of guilt begin to consume me as I saw other students being beat at Berkeley for mobilizing around inequality, as I saw the inhumane and unjust execution of Troy Davis, and as I saw myself murdered again, this time in a young boy in Florida named Trayvon Martin. All of these incidents put me, and many of us, through an existential crisis. The question that I kept asking myself was: What was the point of this Stanford education and privilege? And how can I truly stand in solidarity with the 99 percent when I was in the educational 1 percent?

I implored my fellow students to use our tools and resources to create a more just world. "Who knows," I concluded, "but maybe we were called to graduate from Stanford University for precisely such a time as this."

On June 28, 2012, the City of Stockton filed for bankruptcy. It was the largest city to file in U.S. history, in terms of both debt load and population. In her statement, Mayor Ann Johnston said, "We are extremely disappointed that we have been unable to avoid bankruptcy," but that it had to happen "to get our fiscal house in order." Chapter 9 protection was Stockton's only choice, according to the city manager, after failing to restructure more than seven hundred million dollars of debt with creditors including retirees, city workers, and bondholders.

Until 2008, the housing boom had driven up prices and city revenues, as Stockton became a hot new bedroom community for the San Francisco Bay Area. New development even sprung up in South Stockton, thanks to its proximity to the freeway and the Bay Area jobs beyond it. Median home prices tripled between 1999 and 2005. After the bust, they dropped by 60 percent. Stockton had the second-highest rate of foreclosures in the United States after Las Vegas. More than ninety million dollars were slashed from the budget after 2009, including reducing the police department by 25 percent, cutting the fire department by 30 percent, and slashing pay by as much as 22 percent for some city workers. Still, the cuts had not overcome the deficits.

I was now more certain than ever that my perspective could be of service to the city. No one on the city council at that time was below the age of forty-five nor had personal experience with the hardships that were so common to their constituents. Although the political consultants were fond of telling me to emphasize the bankruptcy of the city as the most important issue, the real people at the doors I knocked on reminded me that the city's fiscal bankruptcy was the result of a bankruptcy in leadership. "Hell, we've been bankrupt out here a long time," was a common refrain.

The neighborhood where I grew up, and the council district I was running to represent, were in zip code 95205. Just four and a half miles and ten minutes away, there was an affluent district with the zip code 95219. The difference in life expectancy between those two areas is ten years! This difference was not the result of personal choices. People did not choose to live in a neighborhood so unsafe they can't go jogging on their own streets for fear of being shot. No one chose to have only liquor stores in their neighborhood, as opposed to grocery stores. Between those two zip codes there is also a seventy-five-thousand-dollar difference in average income and a 30 percent difference in the rates of unemployment. The differences in those two zip codes reveal systemic issues that could not be addressed piecemeal, but required structural changes. The only way to get those structural changes was to discuss those discrepancies as an urgent matter requiring the entire city's attention.

The bankruptcy also attracted the attention of my old rival from student council days, Lange Luntao. After I won the primary, he reached out to congratulate me and to offer his assistance in the lead-up to the general elections. Even in his circles, parents of friends were getting laid off and in dire straits. I didn't particularly welcome the offer—I'd reached out to Lange a few times when I was visiting Harvard, his alma mater, to see if we could grab coffee and catch up, and I'd never received a reply. It rankled that he only got in touch after I won the primary. Lange had grown up in a gated community, in a stable home with both his parents present, and had attended the best public high school in the city, my school's archrival, at least on the football field.

However, Lange had acquired some useful skills while at Harvard. He had been a field volunteer in the Obama campaign, a part-time field manager for a local city council race, and involved in a campaign to flip a congressional seat in Pennsylvania. He'd done his thesis on conservative political movements. He had access to communities in Stockton that were more like the people I knew at Stanford, but whom I didn't know back at home. Lange was smart and talented, and I needed someone with his expertise, so I hired him as my field director.

Although for the primaries only residents in District 6 got to vote for me, the general election in November was citywide. We didn't just have to organize South Stockton; we had to organize Lange's neighborhood, the North—the gated communities; we had to organize the rural areas. We were running against an incumbent Republican in a city that was fairly red, particularly in other districts. I won the primary in a district that was 75 percent Democratic and now had to run citywide in a place that was barely over 50 percent Democratic. I needed Lange to pull off the upset in November.

Right away, Lange came up with a brilliant plan to leverage my youth and mentorship experience by assembling "Reinvent Stockton Organizers," a campaign volunteer base drawn from the young people who stood to most feel the effects of political leadership, either positive or negative, by virtue of the amount of time they had left to live in the community. Our weekend canvasses were civic church meetings with Lange leading the charge and teaching the basics of campaign field organizing to dozens of high school students.

The gated communities of Stockton had the highest rates of voters, but it was hard to make inroads there because you could only get inside with a resident's pass. Lange used his mother's access card to get us in, groups of mostly Black and Brown young folks. He got in trouble with the homeowners association, but he persisted. "It's a public street," was his response. In the end, I had some of the highest rates of support in those neighborhoods.

As I got to know Lange, I understood that he was not simply the spoiled kid I'd taken him for when we first met. Both his parents, his Filipino father and his Nebraska-born mother, had come with their families to the Central Valley for jobs as farmworkers. His dad grew up in Stockton at a time when Filipinos were forced to live in South Stockton. He was a child when the thriving Little Manila neighborhood was destroyed to make way for a freeway in the early 1960s. Both of Lange's parents, Willie and Mary, had gone to college and become teachers in the Stockton Unified School District, and the minute they could afford to do so, when Lange was around twelve years old, they moved to the neighborhood with the best schools for their kids' sakes, which is how they'd ended up in the gated community.

Together we ran a great campaign. Over the course of the next six months, we were able to knock on the door of almost every registered voter in the city: around 100,000 households. If we didn't knock on their door, we made a phone call or sent some form of literature to them.

In canvassing neighborhoods different from the ones I grew up in, I realized how many issues were shared between them. Everyone worried about security—they just had different means by which to ensure it. The wealthy neighborhoods had private security and gated communities to create the feeling of safety they craved, while the less well-off had gates and chain-link fences and guard dogs to create the same feeling. Everyone worried about their children and grandchildren, wanting them to have the opportunity to go to a school like Stanford or to otherwise pursue their dreams. No matter the net worth of the individual, everyone wanted to live in a city that they were proud of and to see something better in their elected leadership.

One evening as I walked the streets near UOP, an older white couple came out of their stately house. "Are you Michael Tubbs?" I heard. They invited me in.

They told me about meeting as students at UOP and falling in love not just with each other, but also with the city they now called home. They offered to organize my precinct list for me so that I wouldn't be lost. "These streets are a little tricky," they said.

As they handed back my list, I asked them if they were voters, rifling through my pages.

"Every election!"

"That's interesting, because you're not on my list of voters to talk to."

They eyed each other knowingly and smiled. "Oh, we're Republicans. We have been our entire lives. But don't worry, we admire and support you."

I bid them good night, elated that our campaign had appeal beyond party lines. People of all leanings were looking for reasons to believe again, and it seemed I could be one of those reasons. They liked my authenticity and that I didn't profess to have easy solutions, but would do the hard work to find lasting ones. I wasn't trying to move Stockton left or right, but forward.

I decided against knocking on any more doors that night, though, turning for home with the black sky as a backdrop. Although a Stanford graduate and a candidate for elected office, I was always cognizant of the fact that I was still a young Black man walking after nightfall in an affluent neighborhood that was not mine. Trayvon Martin had been murdered for less.

Fundraising continued to be my biggest challenge. "We have to raise one hundred K by October to compete," was Nicholas Hatten's mantra. I would smirk or roll my eyes in reply. Not that I disagreed. We needed money for mailings and to pay his and Lange's (admittedly meager) salaries. But I was still uncomfortable doing the asking—until Nicholas confronted me with a come-to-Jesus moment. "There's no way you're going to win and do all the good things that you want to do if you don't have the resources to do it. You can't lead people if you are uncomfortable with asking them to help." I could get behind fundraising as a leadership tool, a way of asking supporters to help be a part of the cause. My doubts quieted going forward.

Yet we were still falling short of our goals. Nicholas mentioned that MC Hammer had an interest in Stockton because he lived in Tracy, a nearby town, and that I should reach out. A tweet led to a phone call in which MC Hammer asked me how much money I needed. Five thousand, I told him, despite the fact that Nicholas had told me our shortfall for the necessary voter mailing was seventy-five hundred. The next day I found myself in the parking lot of In-N-Out talking to MC Hammer about our campaign to Reinvent Stockton. Passersby gawked and asked for a picture with Hammer. I'd have happily acquiesced, but Hammer made sure everyone who got a photo would also support my campaign. As he departed, he handed me an envelope. Inside was a check for exactly the amount we needed but which I had been too uncomfortable to ask for: seventy-five hundred dollars. Shaking my head, I looked up to the heavens saying, "This really is supposed to happen, huh?" I peeled off playing "2 Legit 2 Quit" all the way back to campaign headquarters.

The city's largest newspaper, *The Stockton Record*, would make an endorsement decision after the only debate between myself and Dale Fritchen. Nicholas and Lange were excited by this chance for me to show I thought like a councilman despite my age. They created prep sessions and spent several nights grilling me over city policy, bankruptcy, why I was running, the general plan—all the while critiquing my responses, forcing me to be more concise in my answers.

On the night of the debate, the council chambers were filled with people who were white, over fifty, and mostly supporters of my opponent. Debates for council races are generally cordial, but I went on the attack on the incumbent's record, disputing his statements and making the case that fresh leadership was required to move our city in the direction we deserved. I remarked that Fritchen's lone vote against bankruptcy was his attempt to curry favor from the police and fire unions, and that if he was truly concerned about the city's finances he could've begun coming up with a plan as chair of the budget committee years before. I shared how, despite not being a councilmember, I was already organizing events against violence in the district because Fritchen was missing in action. I remarked that his approach to solving crime—installing light bulbs and suggesting that people read his guide on the importance of locking doors—put too much responsibility on his constituents and too little on him and his colleagues to change environments in which people were snatching purses from old ladies and gold chains from people's necks. I concluded by saying that I didn't have all the answers, but that I would lead a community-rooted team to seek them.

The next day the *Record* ran its endorsement, stating: "Stockton native Michael Tubbs brings not only the cerebral horsepower that got him a Stanford education, but also a street-level understanding of the South City District . . . the energy Tubbs offers is infectious . . . Stockton voters would be well-served by putting Tubbs on the council."

The political establishment remained unmoved. Some councilmembers expressed support, but did not want to publicly endorse a candidate, and the public safety unions claimed I hadn't turned in my application for endorsement despite the fact that I hand-delivered it myself. We were nervous as we entered the weekend before Election Day, Get Out the Vote weekend. We had no funds to do polling, so we had no idea where we stood, besides our own interactions with voters. The week before, I had predicted winning with 60 percent of the vote, a statement the press had picked up, to the frustration of both Nicholas and Lange.

Much of Election Day was spent on getting people to the polls. Anna organized a contingent of volunteers to come down from Stanford, which, combined with the Reinvent Stockton organizers Lange had turned out, formed a volunteer army of one hundred people. At 8:00 P.M. the polls closed, but it was at least an hour after that before we saw the results at a Mexican restaurant a five-minute walk from the first house my mother owned.

Michael Tubbs 60 percent—Dale Fritchen 40 percent.

Michael Tubbs, councilmember-elect for the City of Stockton, District 6.

11

ROSES FROM CONCRETE

There but for the grace of God go I, I thought as I passed the guys who had assembled for the meeting in Stockton's Teen Impact Center. They all looked like me, had backgrounds like mine, and I'd even grown up with some of them. But they were all on one side of the table—the side reserved for the men who had the highest proximity to violent crime—while I took my seat on the other side, just a few months after my swearing-in as councilman for District 6. Also on my side of the table were Stockton police chief Eric Jones, the U.S. attorney, and several parole officers and community leaders. We had invited these men, many of whom had been incarcerated and all of whom had ties to Stockton's gangs, to discuss community safety. Rather than just having the police lecture about law enforcement, the community leaders were there to talk about opportunities that could prevent further harm. In 2012, Stockton led the nation in murders per capita, and had over 150 active gangs and drug trafficking sets. In 2010, the year Donnell was murdered, there were fifty homicides; in 2012 there were seventy-one. I was driven to change this number and to get my city to confront the fact that the root cause was poverty.

The men themselves were an important part of the solution. We wanted them to recognize that the violence had to stop, and we wanted them to remain alive, free, and helping us progress as a city. The air in the room felt thick. In the faces across from me were the fatigue and pain I knew so well, the battle scars of growing up poor and trapped, with fragmented families, in neighborhoods where the only government intervention seemed to be putting more people in jail cells and increasing police presence. In the eyes of these men, I saw outcomes the Summer Success and Leadership Academy was designed to prevent. In their eyes I saw surprise at where I sat, and I saw why I had decided to come back to Stockton in the first place.

I had three minutes to address them, and I had three major points to make.

"Number one, for the city to reach its potential, I need each of you to reach your potential. Number two, it's unacceptable, but the leading cause of death for people like us, between eighteen and thirty-five, in the state of California, is homicides. Not a car accident, not a heart attack, but gun violence. It's unacceptable. I need you to stay alive. You're at risk of being shot or being a shooter, and both of those things are unacceptable to me. And number three, the violence has to stop. It's not easy to make a change, but we are committed to providing you with opportunity. We'll walk with you."

I concluded: "I get it. It's not fair, you didn't choose to live in this community with no opportunities. I understand. I also understand how angry your kid will feel growing up without their father. I did that; it's not fun. How sad your family will be at your funeral, or what you'll feel at theirs. I've done that too.

"So, let's not make a bad situation worse."

By the time I sat down I was drained. I imagined that I had spoken not just to the men present, but to my father twenty-three years ago, to Donnell and his killer two years ago, to my classmates and neighbors in middle school and high school. I wanted them all to know that the setup was real, that their lives mattered, and that we needed them to turn the city around. I was surprised that my raw emotions about my family were at the surface, but I allowed them to stay. I was angry, I was passionate, and I was resolute that we would upset the setup.

The police chief took it from there. Eric Jones had taken over as police chief shortly before my election, just after the city's bankruptcy declaration. White, mid-forties, clean-shaven, a computer science major and data-geek, he had started his service with the Stockton Police Department in the 1990s as a beat cop at a time when success was defined as the highest number of arrests. Over time, he realized that the official strategies were reducing safety while increasing fear and violence, and he began searching for models that would rebuild trust between community members and the police.

By design, I'd had very limited interaction with law enforcement as a young man, as I told Chief Jones. Still, Eric and I just clicked. He'd reached out while I was campaigning for my seat and said he hoped I would win because what I was saying resonated with him—despite the police union's outright opposition to me. He told me: "I think poverty is the issue in this city, and I don't think my cops are sufficient to handle the problems we have with poverty." He struck me as a listener and a strategist who could act quickly when he saw promising data.

After Chief Jones spoke about ending violence being the top community priority and of his desire to see the men remain alive and free and not in police custody, there was a slide show by the district attorney about people who had been recently incarcerated and the sentences they received, including a seventeen-year-old boy getting twenty-five years to life on gun and drug charges. Another brutal reminder of my father. After the meeting was over, several of the invitees approached me. "You a councilman?" they said, still in disbelief. They took selfies with me. One guy said he wanted to be mayor, and I offered that he come by city hall and shadow me for a day. Then a guy I knew from recreation league basketball motioned me over to talk with him.

"I don't know why I'm here, bro, I have a construction job. I've been good for like two years. I have a kid, I'm not . . ."

I said, "Then it's not for you. It's for people in your crew or people you used to run with."

The invites to the meeting went out to guys we could reach. If they weren't directly shooting, we knew that they were one degree of separation from the violence. They were all young men under twenty-seven who had been incarcerated. All had shot or been shot at. All had lost someone to violence. The majority of them did not grow up with their fathers, most of whom were incarcerated or dead. We were inviting their leadership in helping the city pioneer this new approach to achieving safety. We were inviting them to take advantage of the mentorship offered by our Peacekeepers, street outreach workers who could connect them to jobs and counseling and make sure they had the case management support needed to make changes. We were inviting them to be part of a leadership council that would advise the police chief and the city council on strategies and activities we could employ to create safety. We were inviting them to be part of the solution.

"To inspire a nobler civic life, to fulfill justice, to serve the people," were the words I saw every time I walked up the steps of Stockton City Hall and looked up at the top of the building. To this day, they serve as a motivation, a credo, and a reminder of why the hours I spent in the council chambers were worth it. During my first weeks as a councilmember, I clung to those words as I found myself battling feelings of inferiority, questioning whether I could be effective in my new role. There weren't many models of councilmembers in cities trying to recover from bankruptcy and the nation's highest per capita homicide rate. Especially twenty-two-year-old ones representing a council district of fifty thousand people.

My anxiety was despite the throngs of people who had turned out for my swearing-in—so many that city officials moved the ceremony to the larger county building to accommodate the crowds, and even so hundreds were left outside the three-hundred-person-capacity chambers. I struggled to make it on time, inundated with requests for pictures and hugs from well-wishers. My mother, aunt, and grandmother, their eyes glistening with pride, joined me at the dais as my mom led me in the oath of office. Newly sworn in, I launched into unprepared remarks ending with "Weeping may endure for a night, but joy comes in the morning. Good morning, Stockton."

My imposter syndrome hung on until the first city council meeting. We were tasked with interviewing and appointing a replacement for Councilmember Susan Eggman, who had just won the election to the California State Assembly. As I listened to the questions posed to the candidates, I realized the mayor and the vice-mayor had a replacement in mind, because they were giving her softballs. The candidate I believed was the best choice got harder questions and wasn't the most persuasive speaker. I racked my mind for what could be done to elevate her and derail the mayor and vice-mayor's fix. I asked the mayor's nominee, Planning Commissioner Christina Fugazi, a question I thought would reveal her true motives, rather than letting her say what others wanted to hear. "Given the financial situation of the city, where would you propose making cuts?"

Fugazi responded with what she wouldn't cut, which amounted to everything, and then said she didn't have access to the city budget, so was unable to answer. Previous to my question she had claimed that she was always overprepared, and I seized on her inconsistency. "With all due respect, planning commissioner, the city's budget is a public document and is online at Stocktonca.gov. Even without knowing the budget, as an applicant for city council, you should have some idea of what the city funds, even if you don't know the exact amount of funding." Mayor Silva cut me off, saying my time for questions was done, but two other councilmembers capitalized on my line of questioning. By the time Fugazi finished, it was apparent that the candidate I supported was the superior choice. The council welcomed Dyane Burgos, a thirty-two-year-old Latina social worker, on a 5–2 vote, with the mayor and vice-mayor dissenting. As I was leaving the meeting, veteran councilmembers thanked me for my questioning.

Mayor Silva, however, was seething. "I thought we were on the same team," he shot at me as I exited the chamber.

"I'm on Team Stockton," I replied.

* * *

Calling himself "the People's Mayor," Anthony Silva, the former school board chair and leader of the local Boys & Girls Clubs of America, was new to city hall, like me. Also like me, he had won his election against an incumbent, beating Ann Johnston, during whose tenure the city had declared bankruptcy.

His tenure as mayor would be described by several media outlets as "Silva's Circus." There were his harmless-yet-ineffective press stunts, like donning a gladiator helmet at the close of his first State of the City address, or the night he slept in a cardboard box under a freeway overpass, telling reporters he was there to give homeless people hope, or organizing a twelve-hour prayer rally during which he formally gave God the honorary key to the city. One of his ideas was to import manatees from Florida to the Port of Stockton so they would eat the invasive hyacinths that were obstructing the waterway. Not only would transporting this endangered species be illegal, but manatees require tropical temperatures and would have perished in the colder waters during the first winter in Stockton.

In response to both the severity of the issues and the mayor's chaotic leadership, I asserted myself in council meetings. I asked a lot of questions—tough questions, pointed questions, unrelenting questions—until everyone in the room was looking at me like: *Whoa. This kid is not here to play.*

At one meeting during my early months, the mayor asked us to vote on his crime plan without sharing the proposal with us beforehand. A community leader who had been working closely with the mayor got me the plan ahead of time anyway, knowing how deeply I cared about the issue. I read the plan and found it to be untenable. The mayor proposed a restricted tax that would go just to police salaries and staffing, to be overseen by former New York City police chief Bill Bratton, the mayor's planned replacement for Chief Jones. I agreed with the goal of reducing crime, but didn't agree with this solution. I wanted to see more emphasis on prevention, as opposed to the broken windows theory espoused by Bratton, and wanted to make sure we also had the resources to fund our exit from bankruptcy.

Worried, I made copies of the plan and made sure every councilmember had one in their mailbox before the meeting. The then–city manager eyed me warily during our check-in meeting and asked me how in the hell I'd gotten a copy. I smiled and said I wasn't at liberty to share that, but here you go. He smiled back and said, "You're going places, Tubbs. You're too smart for your own good."

At the council meeting, the mayor was apoplectic. He thought someone had broken into his office and stolen his "top secret" plan. He did not even suspect that I, the young Black kid on the council, would have the wherewithal and connections to get ahold of the plan and disseminate it. Soon it was a moot point: the mayor's proposal was rejected after a council meeting that lasted well past midnight. Shortly thereafter, a plan for public safety was developed in consultation with the city manager, police chief, city council, and community organizations and leaders that then went to the public for a vote. The plan took the form of a tax measure, known as Measure A and B, 66 percent of which would go to public safety and 33 percent to backfill our general fund and build up city services.

As part of the negotiations, I successfully lobbied for the creation of an Office of Violence Prevention to institutionalize our need to address violence before it happened. Chief Jones and I spent most of my first year with our public safety consultant, Stewart Wakeling, designing that office, from scope to staffing. Occasionally we disagreed, most staunchly on the question of whether the office should report directly to the police chief or work with the police department, but report to the city manager. I argued that the latter would help the office to maintain its independence and also to elevate its stature; eventually, Chief Jones relented, agreeing to disagree.

As the new crime plan was prepared for a citywide vote, I was nominated by the council and other city leaders to have my name on the ballot as one of the prominent endorsers of the measure. Soon after, I received a call from the head of the city's business council, Jane Butterfield. Jane, who came from old Stockton, was a fairly wealthy white woman from a family of public servants and barrier breaking in her own right as the first woman to serve as the president of a bank in the entire Central Valley of California. Jane called and asked if I was indeed signing on to the ballot measure, as she respected my leadership and was asked to do the same. I told her I was, and she replied, "Okay, I'll sign too." Our relationship continued to deepen, to the point that later that year, when she was named Stocktonian of the Year, Jane asked if I would officiate and present her the award. A lot of people were surprised, and heads turned when I showed up to sit at the head table at the Stockton Golf & Country Club for the ceremony.

I knew how this game was played, I realized. It was all about relationships and information, molding consensus, getting to yes. In running citywide for my council seat, I had already developed deep relationships with unexpected people. My youth was also an asset in this regard, as people often saw me as a novelty rather than a threat and were perhaps more willing to work with me than with someone they could more easily categorize. As a result, I became close with the activists, the business community, the artistic and rapper community, the teachers, the superintendent of schools and the Stockton School Board members, my colleagues on the city council, and the police chief. I got input from all sides and was able to gain a 360-view of the city's interests.

On the council dais, I became a bridge between the two other younger people of color on the council—Dyane Burgos, whom we had appointed, and Moses Zapien, a mid-thirties Latino lawyer—and the veteran councilmembers who had made the tough decision to declare bankruptcy: Kathy Miller and Elbert Holman, both over sixty. With this group, I believed, we would be able to move the city forward despite the mayor's antics.

"Son, I don't care about Stanford. I don't care about Oprah. I care about what you can do for this community," Ms. Delgado informed me, her hands on her hips, her eyes sharp behind her dark glasses.

My first meeting with STAND, Stocktonians Taking Action to Neutralize Drugs, was not going quite as planned. I was hoping to address an issue near the top of my district's agenda: the matter of New Grand Save, the liquor store on Airport Way across the street from the Dorothy Jones Community Center, where Nana had her office. For twenty years, basically my entire lifetime, women in the neighborhood had been protesting the liquor store and the culture of uninhibited drug-dealing that it magnetized. Around the time I was born, four women of color had founded STAND, and ever since they had been railing at city hall, speaking candidly to city officials about the neglect in their neighborhood. Ms. Delgado was not afraid to rail at me, too.

When I earnestly asked her and the other *abuelas* what needed to be done, they took me outside and pointed down the street. New Grand Save. On any given day at every hour, the parking lot was full, not with patrons or parked cars, but with young and middle-aged Black men hanging out, betting on dice, playing music, drinking out of tall cans. Sporadic violence came every time the heat or their tempers rose. Despite the blatant drug sales and recurring gun violence over the years, the promises of city officials and court battles had changed nothing. I promised the grandmothers it would be one of my top priorities.

If South Stockton can be designated an official Promise Zone, I thought, *and receive some of the grant money that the Obama Administration was infusing into neighborhoods like ours, that could move the dial.* As an intern in the White House, I had seen the development of the Promise Zones initiative, and as a councilmember I saw the impact the designation had on Los Angeles, San Antonio, and Philadelphia in their efforts to confront generational poverty. I set about organizing to make that happen, in the process creating the Reinvent South Stockton Coalition. This coalition was designed to bring all relevant partners together to focus on collective solutions to longstanding problems and to ensure that South Stockton would always have a voice at the table, no matter who was in office. Although he was working on a Fulbright Scholarship in the Philippines, I convinced Lange to come back and help build the coalition. With city government staffing one-third leaner because of the bankruptcy, Lange and I wrote the application for Promise Zone status ourselves. The bankruptcy made it difficult for the city to do any more than it was currently doing, staffing a bare maintenance-level government. We were close, in the end, but without a true city government partner we missed the designation.

To find out other priorities of the constituents of my district, I worked with the Reinvent South Stockton Coalition to launch a community assessment. It felt like being on the campaign trail again, knocking on doors, asking about people's concerns and needs, and inviting them to a meeting at Van Buskirk to which about four hundred people showed up. Out of these efforts I learned that the most pressing need was a health clinic to serve low-income, uninsured, and undocumented residents.

Like a miracle, a space for the clinic soon presented itself. As I was touring the district, I visited the Dorothy Jones Center. I noticed an unused space in the back and asked about it.

"Oh, there was supposed to be a clinic here ten years ago, a health clinic," a Dorothy Jones staff member told me.

There was a dormant health clinic sitting vacant and unused for a decade, while the community's greatest need was for a health clinic? I asked what stood in the way of getting it up and running.

"Well, councilman, we don't know anyone who can run a health clinic," the staffer said.

As it happened, I was already in touch with a group called Community Medical Centers. I sent them a message and asked if they could make it happen. Six months later, the health clinic was open.

At first, we could only afford to have it open a few hours every week, so I reached out to the local Rotary Club in hopes of getting their support for an expansion of hours. I worked closely with a gentleman named Bob Foy, who has since passed. Bob Foy was a bow tie–wearing, wealthy, San Jose State Spartan booster. He was very conservative, an uber-Republican. As we signed the final resolution to open the clinic for full service, forty-eight hours per week, Bob said, "Councilman Tubbs, I want to give you a gift."

He presented me with a pen. It was an O'Reilly Factor Lifetime Membership pen. I was startled by this keepsake from the Fox News icon, Bill O'Reilly, infamous for his racist stereotypes and anti-immigrant sentiment. *What kind of commitment gets you an O'Reilly Factor Lifetime Membership gift?* I thought.

Outwardly, I just smiled and replied, "You know I'm going to sign some really progressive legislation with this pen."

His response: "Councilman Tubbs, I'm just trying to be a good neighbor."

That moment reinforced what I had learned in community organizing, that there are no permanent friends and no permanent enemies—just permanent issues. And that change often comes with a coalition of unlikely allies.

My mom always left the check-cashing place looking a little more tired than she went in. That had confused me growing up, as I thought the check-cashing place was like a bank, and that people were generally happy when they received money. I was never allowed to go inside when we stopped by; I just stayed in the car waiting for her to trudge out.

When I was twelve, she finally came out with a smile. Confused, I asked, "Momma, what's so different about this time than the other times?"

"What do you mean?" she said.

"You usually come out of here lookin' mad."

"Oh!" She laughed and said, "I'm smiling this time because this is the last time I'll ever go to a check-cashing place. When you are older, do not come here. They'll trap you. They prey on people who need money by charging extra money for letting them get their money quicker, so you end up with less money than you had," she explained. "It's like a drug; you get your money so fast, but sometimes I'd have to go right back in there and borrow some more because I didn't have enough to make ends meet," she continued. "You in that line and you embarrassed because you don't want people to see you there. Never come here, seriously."

I've been suspicious of check cashing, or payday lending and cash advance places, ever since.

Accordingly, I was determined to find a way to increase the number of banks in South Stockton. My district was a "bank desert," an area with inadequate banking services, which allowed for the proliferation of alternative financial services like payday lenders. These predatory institutions trapped many of my constituents in cycles of debt and made it hard for them to build assets for themselves and their families, charging interest rates as high as 600 percent.

I asked Michael Duffy, the president of the Financial Center Credit Union, the bank that my family used, to lunch one day to pick his brain. "Mike, what would it take to get a bank in South Stockton?"

"No one's ever asked me that before," he said.

Time and time again, I was finding that you could sometimes get results just by asking the right questions. People assume that the status quo is the way it is because the question has been asked and answered, but often the question has never even been raised.

Then he said: "I've been thinking about it since before 2008, but then the recession hit. You know, the timing is right. I'm going to do it." And just like that, plans for a credit union in South Stockton were underway.

12

UPSET THE SETUP

In Stockton, every councilmember represents a district of about fifty thousand people. Despite that responsibility, the job pays only twenty-two thousand dollars a year, not enough for a full-time salary despite the full-time demands of the job. I was neither independently wealthy nor retired, so I had to figure something else out. I worked on council matters from before dawn until 8:00 A.M. and filled my evenings and weekends with council meetings and constituent requests. I was hardly able to see Anna more than twice a month, who, for her part, was busy completing the second half of her undergraduate studies back at Stanford. All the while, I also had a "day job": teaching full-time, every weekday.

I spent my first year as a councilmember as the interim director of the Community Involvement Program at UOP, but decided not to renew my time there—academia had more politics to deal with than city hall. In 2013 and 2014, I made good on my promise to my summer school kids and returned to teach full-time at Langston Hughes Academy.

The sixth and seventh graders I had taught the summer

before I left for college were now eleventh and twelfth graders, and my students. My schedule was brutal, as I was tasked with creating the curriculum for our Early College Program, a program through which the students could take community college courses on campus. In addition to creating the curriculum from scratch, I also taught five subjects a day, a different course each hour: U.S. government, Introduction to Sociology, ethnic studies, speech, and debate.

The classroom gave me the space to not only teach but to apply theories to the work I was doing as a councilmember. The kids really loved my Intro to Sociology course, as I made sure it was rooted in their experiences of growing up in Stockton. We talked about socialization and the impact of environment, about violence and its causes. I drew upon the lessons I learned in writing my honor's thesis and studying Paulo Freire's *Pedagogy of the Oppressed,* using rap lyrics and popular culture as case studies. I stressed critical thinking, wanting to teach my students how to think, as opposed to what to think. They loved it.

"Brenda's got a baby, but Brenda's barely got a brain," began the final project instructions for the Intro to Sociology course. I had them use examples from Tupac's "Brenda's Got a Baby" to determine the extent to which they believed structural causes versus personal agency were the cause of the outcomes we saw in our society. On day two of our final exam, sensing that the essay I'd assigned on the topic was not going to showcase all that the students had learned, I divided them up into teams. They would debate each other using evidence from their essays—team structure versus team agency. I invited the principal to watch, and he was amazed. The students were passionate, were taking it personally, and were backing up their arguments with more logic and evidence than I heard on Tuesday nights at city hall, as I told them. "You've set a high bar," said Principal Solina, "but every single student is reaching it, Mr. Tubbs."

In every class I was determined to deliver the lessons that had proven consequential for my own intellectual development, without dumbing anything down. In my Introduction to Ethnic Studies courses, the syllabus was comparable to the courses I took at Stanford, a fact my students took in with hoots and groans. Week 1 was "Race as a Social Construct." Week 3: "Intersectionality." Week 5: "Privilege and Power." Week 7: "Stereotypes." The next courses were "The Impact of a Racial Society on Media" (Week 8), "Education" (Week 9), and "Crime" (Week 10). Weeks twelve through seventeen focused on different nonwhite identities and experiences: Native, Asian, Mexican, and Black. Class by class, I would seek to meet my students where they were, without sacrificing the truths I had to share.

First period started at 8:22 A.M., although I could never seem to get there before 8:30 A.M. The girls were screaming with laughter as they entered my classroom even later than that. I stepped right up to block their path. "Wait. Where are we right now? At the club?"

"Sorry, Mr. Tubbs."

"I appreciate your apology. But when you hit this door, we have to code switch, okay. We're code switching . . . performing. We're going to perform as students for the next hour."

My students had so much potential, and I viewed part of

my role as educator as teaching them ways of being, ways to maintain the essence of who they were while still learning how to read a room and act accordingly. You can be the same, but you can't act the same everywhere, I told them repeatedly.

Anayiah was loud, but she was brilliant. She had skipped a grade, and she loved competition, excelling at the quizzes I made up that interspersed subject matter fill-in-the-blanks with fill-in-the-blanks for song lyrics.

I turned to the rest of the students. "In today's episode of 'The Wire,'" I said with a grin, which was my customary way of starting class, "Mr. Tubbs tries to teach his students about . . ." They didn't understand the reference, so the joke only landed with me. Eventually, I showed them an episode of "The Wire," season 4, set in an unruly classroom in Baltimore. They were aghast. "Mr. Tubbs, you play too much! We were not that bad, not that bad, uh-uh, uh-uh!"

Jesus had also skipped a grade. He was no longer the quiet, athletic sixth grader in my brother's class, possessed of great potential. Now he was a teenager with a little swagger, always sure to accessorize the school uniform with new Jordans and a Gucci belt. He tried to hide his intelligence, but I knew better. I recognized myself at that age in him and began to understand why some of my teachers may have found me annoying. The ability to traverse different worlds, the ability to just kick it, but also to perform in class, Jesus had that mastered. He was the best basketball player in the school, knew all the pop culture references, listened exclusively to trap hip hop and had straight A's. I appreciated his balancing act and recognized his hustle. So I put him on notice.

After his first week in my class, I pulled him aside. "I'm going to be very unfair to you."

"What do you mean?"

"Well, because I know what you're capable of. What's an A for everyone else will be a B for you. What won't give you an A at Stanford won't get an A in my class." For his first paper in sociology I gave him a B-. He was devastated. He stayed after class and asked me what he could do to improve. He took in the feedback and got an A on every paper after that. Once, when I was late arriving, I found him leading the class, reviewing the lessons and the reading I had given on police reform and stop-and-frisk the day before.

Although he hadn't been at Langston Hughes when I first met his classmates, Donovon became someone I invested a lot of time in. Donovon was white, with an Eminem kind of cool in an environment overwhelmingly of classmates of color. He played basketball, he loved hip hop, and loved to share that he only dated girls of color. The class period was never enough for him; he lingered in my room, asking questions.

"Donovon, bro, I got to go to city hall."

"Mr. Tubbs, I just need thirty more minutes."

I was often late for meetings after school because I was helping Donovon. He was so hungry, so determined, so eager, and I wanted to do everything I could to match his effort with the resources he needed.

It turned out that Donovon didn't have a computer and was homeless, living out of his car or couch surfing at just seventeen years old. I took him under my wing. I marveled at his persistence, his willingness to do his best on the challenging assignments I gave him, his desire to go to college—so much so that I let him take my work laptop to use for his papers and college applications and bring it back in time for me to teach the next day. Donovon was special in part because he didn't try to be Black or Latino. He just was him. "I'm a product of my environment, a culture of many that makes me who I am," he explained in his college admissions essay.

None of the cast of characters that starred in my teaching career was more challenging, energizing, and, frankly, more entertaining, than Isaac. We had connected during my first stint at Langston Hughes, and our bond and struggle continued upon my return. What Isaac lacked in academic skills, he made up for in street smarts: he was charismatic, popular, and an athlete to boot, even as he navigated a tough home situation, as he didn't know his father at all. But some of his choices would spark major conflict between us.

He was a terrible student, terrible because he had missed some fundamentals along the way and no one had noticed and helped him to catch up. He also had trouble focusing; he was lazy with the stuff that didn't come easy. But he wanted to make me happy, so he made an effort in class. The final term paper was a big deal—eight to twelve pages, half the grade for the class. Isaac came in with a dilapidated, not-even-a-real laptop, one of those children's toy versions. You would've thought he was going for an Academy Award, the way he pulled the thing out his bag and attempted to turn it on, groaning and sighing. I ignored him, angry and amused, but not about to validate his performance. As the bell rang, I asked if he had his term paper. He brought back the dramatics: "Oh, Mr. Tubbs, I don't know what happened, my laptop broke."

"Isaac. As much time and effort as you spent coming up with this old, dusty laptop and doing this whole hour-long, dramatic monologue about how it doesn't work, you could've written your damn paper, bro. I'm going to give you another week. You need to finish it so you can pass my class." He wrote his paper—or someone did.

My most serious confrontation with Isaac happened outside school. Driving past Maya Angelou Library around 10:00 P.M. one night on my way home after a long day of teaching and council meetings, I noticed a couple of high schoolers hanging on the corner. Ordinarily, I would have made a note and checked in with the police chief to see what was happening in the area, but one of the students looked familiar.

I knew that hoodie.

Seeing Isaac on the corner in my council district after he'd taken up so much of my time and care at Langston Hughes was too much, and I pulled over and jumped out the car. "Isaac?" I said with more bass in my voice than usual. "What are you doing on my corners?"

"Just hanging out, Mr. Tub-Tubbs," he stumbled, clearly shocked.

I told him how it was in no uncertain terms. "Listen, I don't need to know what you're doing, but I tell you this: I'm not going to spend all day teaching you, then spend all night trying to make your city safe, to have you disrespecting me by standing on this corner doing whatever it is—I think I have an idea. Do you understand me?"

He nodded, sheepishly, avoiding my gaze and glancing at his friends.

"Let me see you out here again, I guarantee I'll call the cops. A hundred percent. You know I know the police chief personally. I might have him come up and have a conversation with you, Isaac. I'll do it with a smile on my face, too. Because this is disrespectful to me and to your future."

"Okay, Mr. Tubbs." I heard his boys laughing in the distance when I got in the car. "Nah, man. That's Mr. Tubbs. He crazy. But he coo," I heard Isaac say.

I never saw Isaac on that corner again.

Teaching was a labor of love, both fulfilling and draining. I thought of my students as peers of my high school self and wanted to show up for them in ways that I wished my educators had shown up for me when I was younger. I brought lunches, mentored, attended games, and hosted college admissions workshops. As I had with the Phoenix Scholars during college, I worked intensively with several students on their personal essays, including Anayiah, Jesus, and Donovon. It was incredibly gratifying when Anayiah was accepted by both the University of Chicago and Howard University with full scholarships; Jesus was accepted by the University of California at Berkeley with generous financial aid; and Donovon was accepted by the University of California at Santa Cruz. The whole senior class took a trip to Santa Cruz that spring, and I was proud to escort Donovon on a tour of the school, with Jesus in tow.

My time at Langston Hughes gave me the opportunity to work directly with students who were contending with the issues that had driven me back to Stockton, namely structural violence and poverty. During my time there, what I had sensed during my first stint became even more apparent: that our kids needed someone to believe in them, to go the extra mile, and that sharing their background and identity helped me to reach and guide them. Teaching also allowed me to work through the survivor's guilt that still gnawed at me. On many days, I felt what I accomplished as a teacher was at least as meaningful as my work on the city council. On other days, both roles seemed not enough as the challenges still arose, trauma was still ever-present, and roses were still being forced to grow from the toxic environment of concrete.

The Maya Angelou Library looked no different from how I remembered it when it provided me refuge as a child and introduced me to James Baldwin during my teen years. In an effort to create that environment for other young people, I started a summer book club and hosted it there. I chose books that I hoped would empower readers and broaden their perspectives, texts that featured characters of color and probably weren't going to be part of their school canon. I chose books that I wanted to read.

We read *The Other Wes Moore* by Wes Moore, and *Buck* by M. K. Asante. I was as tough about book club as I was when I taught class—if anyone hadn't done the reading, or missed a meeting, we were going to have a conversation. It was part of my driving home the message that half of succeeding at something was showing up, whether that meant voting, attending a town hall, or coming to book club. The book club usually attracted about ten youths, student government types, but also students whose parents made them attend, and a few I roped in after finding them loitering in the library. The incentives were modest: pizza, camaraderie, and a trip to UOP on the last day to have a book seminar on a college campus. It never ceased to surprise me how many students from Stockton had never been on UOP campus, or even knew there was a top-100 university in their city.

Zack was forced to come to book club by his mother. A frail kid, short, with very dark skin and a raspy voice, he didn't enjoy reading all that much. After the first couple of weeks, though, he began to look forward to our meetings. He participated, he journaled like everyone else in the book club, and he said he actually liked the story of *Buck*. His passion was football, but he wasn't a natural; he had yet to find anything he was exceptional at. When you're trying to break out of poverty in a place like Stockton, being exceptional at something is helpful, whether it's being the best student, the best basketball player, the best rapper.

One day before a book club session, I was in conversation with the police chief about a young boy being shot in my council district over a purebred pit bull puppy. He didn't give me a name, and I had no idea who it was. The next day, Zack came to book club wearing a cast on his leg, explaining to me how upset he was that he was not going to be able to play football this upcoming year. Before I could ask him what happened, he volunteered that he wasn't able to do the reading for the week.

"Zack, what happened?" I asked, thinking he had hurt himself at practice.

"I was shot two days ago. I didn't read the book, but I'm here, I showed up."

I couldn't breathe I was in such disbelief. I was angry at what he had endured, but I was also incredibly proud. I gave Zack a huge hug, telling him, "You keep showing up, there's going to be books about you." He smiled and asked for pizza.

Zack's incident was reminiscent of an experience I had while reading to Dr. Martin Luther King Elementary School students for Dr. Martin Luther King, Jr. Day during the campaign. In the midst of door knocking and phone banking, I wanted to include events that our volunteers could continue to do even after the campaign was over. Reading to students was my favorite reminder of what was at stake.

After introducing myself to the elementary school class, I pulled out the book I had selected: a picture book about Dr. Martin Luther King, Jr. I tried to move through the page about Dr. King's assassination quickly, as I didn't feel equipped to talk to seven-year-olds about death. But immediately a hand went up and a child said: "Mr. Tubbs, my uncle got shot." The child said it so matter of factly that I assumed the uncle had lived, and I replied with, "Violence is horrible. I'm glad he survived."

"No, he died."

Another child's hand went up and he recounted how someone in his neighborhood "got shot." Before I could formulate a response, the students began almost competing with each other, popcorn style, telling about the people they had known who had been shot. I grew quiet to maintain my composure. I felt heavy and helpless. If these kids were experiencing such trauma in first grade, what did the other eleven years of schooling have in store for them?

I finished the book, talked about Dr. King's dream, and then asked the children about their dream for Stockton. With as much energy as they'd recounted stories of shootings, they dreamed up a community with lots of books and ice cream, clean streets, and no violence.

Both the dais and the classroom taught me that charity was not justice, and programs were not policy. I felt challenged to think deeper about how to address the ills that had made me return to Stockton in the first place.

I found myself circling back to reimagining public safety. After ride alongs, town halls, working on the new crime-reduction plan, and establishing the Office of Violence Prevention, I still felt that the police in and of themselves were an inadequate response to issues rooted in poverty.

In 2014, a couple of months before the murder of Michael Brown and the national emergence of the Black Lives Matter movement, Chief Jones and I were talking about building community trust and transparency. I suggested what I thought would be politically feasible: a civilian review board made up of council-appointed citizens who would have the authority to hold the police department accountable. The chief liked the idea, but countered with body cameras. He had read about a town in Idaho that had made them mandatory in 2011, and Rialto, a Southern California city one-third of the size of Stockton, which had introduced them in early 2012. In Rialto, there was solid data: the number of complaints filed against cops dropped 88 percent compared with the previous twelve months, while use of force fell nearly 60 percent during the same period.

I knew it would be a stretch to do both at the same time and wanted to make sure we focused on something likely to pass so that we could build momentum for a reform agenda. "You think we can get body cameras?!"

He thought so. I proposed that we take it to the city council, get the four necessary votes, and steamroll it through, but Chief Jones felt it was important to get the police department and the union on board first. It was the longer and more difficult route; the police union hadn't supported my campaign. But the chief called a meeting with the union leadership, and then another and another. Gradually, over the course of 2014, he was able to mold a consensus. In January of 2015, the police union president and I held a press conference to announce that Stockton, California, was going to be the first city in our county of San Joaquin to put body cameras on our officers.

As both a councilmember and an educator, I learned a lesson that I am still relearning: it might take more time, it might be messier, but it is vital to make people feel ownership of change that will affect them. Bring people in, and they will implement solutions with commitment. As the adage goes, "If you want to go fast, go alone. If you want to go far, go together."

13

KEYS TO THE CITY

A few months after our conversation about landing a bank in South Stockton, Michael Duffy invited me to lunch. I assumed he wanted help with the planning department or some other bureaucratic hurdle. Such requests were becoming a large part of the job. Instead, he spread out an architectural design on the Thai restaurant's table.

"What's that?" I asked. Duffy excitedly updated me on all the progress he and his team had made, finishing with a formal invitation for me to give remarks at the grand opening of the Financial Credit Union in South Stockton, the building on the paper between us. I high-fived him like we had just won an NBA championship.

Momentum was building for me personally as well. During the campaign, two Stanford classmates had recorded material for a documentary they titled *True Son* because I referred to myself in campaign materials as a "True Son" of Stockton. They emailed me to tell me that the film was to premiere at the Tribeca Film Festival and was going to play in theatres in Los Angeles and New York. I was beginning to feel not only blessed but slightly invincible—as if a page had turned and the rest of my life was going to be nothing but winning. I should have been more careful, more mindful that life is made of both peaks and valleys. But I was loving the mountaintop.

The night before the grand opening of the credit union, October 18, I shared the good news with a friend who suggested we head up to Sacramento for bar hopping to celebrate. In my role as a young Black elected official, I was always cognizant of avoiding the reputation of a party boy, and only went out like other twenty-four-year-olds: sparingly. The credit union and the documentary seemed like the perfect time to make an exception.

"Okay, can you pick me up from my house?" I asked him.

"No, dude. You live way on the other side of town. I'm closer to Sacramento. Just come over and park here."

I drove to his house and left my car there. We agreed that I would take us one way if he handled the return trip; I planned on enjoying myself and did not want to be the designated driver. Once in Sacramento, into a couple rounds of Hennessey shots and Coronas, I texted several friends in Sacramento to ask if I could crash at their place. Two different friends wrote back to offer me a room, but then my phone died and I couldn't follow through. Come 2:30 A.M., I had my apprehensions because my friend had been drinking with me, but he insisted he was good to drive us back to Stockton. The grand opening of the bank was happening at 9:30 A.M.

At around 3:30 A.M. on October 19, 2014, we pulled into his driveway, and my friend asked if I wanted to just stay there and sleep until I had to go to the event. But his father was a pastor. My pride wouldn't let me be drunk on the couch of a pastor's house. After all, I was a councilmember.

I got in my car and took off. Admittedly, I'm not a great driver even when sober; I have a terrible tendency to multi-task, which leaves less than my full attention for the road. On this occasion I was far from sober, although I believed I was enough so to drive. On the highway, while searching for the right song and adjusting my heater, I changed lanes without signaling. The music was too loud for me to hear the sirens, but I couldn't ignore the glare of red and blue lights. I pulled over, horrified. *What if everything I've worked for ends here,* I thought.

I took a deep breath as the California Highway Patrol officer approached my car. I resolved to accept whatever consequences were about to come without mentioning that I was a councilmember. I also knew to be low-key and extra deferential because it was dark and the freeway was practically empty, and I didn't want a DUI to turn me into a hashtag because of an officer-involved shooting. The officer asked me if I had been drinking and I responded yes, but hours earlier; I felt good to drive now, I'd just neglected to put on my blinkers. He asked me to step out the car to do a field test, which I thought I passed with flying colors. (The police report documents that I did, in fact, fail.) I agreed to take a Breathalyzer. I was above the limit. Almost double: .137. The officer handcuffed me and we got on our way to the station.

Sitting in the back of the cruiser, I felt powerless and small. Here I was, fulfilling the grim prophecy I had been told growing up, that I would end up arrested and in jail one day. I thought about my father, who was the same age I now was, twenty-four, when he received his third strike. I never felt more empathy for him than in that moment. To add insult to injury, October 19, the day I was arrested, was his birthday.

I knew I had more to offer than the decisions I had made

that night. I hoped desperately that I would be given a second chance.

Maybe my father, too, had deserved another chance.

In the booking area, I could hear some of the officers whispering and snickering as I stood on the block and took my mug shot. One couldn't resist the urge and said, "You're not Councilman Tubbs, are you?"

"Yes, I am," I responded quietly, "and I am so sorry."

The officer seemed to soften. "I appreciate how you didn't come in here trying to big-time."

"Man, I did something wrong. I was over the limit," I said. The same officer escorted me to my cell, where my accommodation for the night was an uncomfortable green chair surrounded by other people who had been arrested for DUIs. "The Dog Whisperer" played incessantly on the TV as I sat with my thoughts.

I was at a loss for how I would explain what had happened to my family, and to Anna, who was studying in the UK. I figured there would be calls for me to resign; I wondered if I would be forced to, and how this would impact my employment as an educator. My anxieties fought each other—and the lingering Hennessey and Coronas—until I finally dozed off.

At 8:00 A.M., I was told to make a call for someone to pick me up. I contacted my aunt Tasha, knowing my mom would be far too emotional, and an argument was the last thing I needed at the moment. Tasha didn't say much on the phone except, "Okay. I love you, I am on my way."

Thirty minutes later, she pulled up to the county jail with my mom, nana, and little brother in tow. My mom had her head in her hands, and Nana wanted to pray as soon as I got in the car. It was eerily quiet, as if someone had passed. In a sense someone had—the Michael Tubbs who, at least in his family's eyes, had it all figured out. The "True Son" who didn't need any more help or forgiveness.

They dropped me off at my house. I kept the lights dark, charged my phone, and sent texts to give people a heads-up: the police chief, the city manager, a couple of councilmembers I trusted, and finally Michael Duffy, who had been asking where I was all morning, and was I okay. I was too embarrassed and too exhausted to make the 9:30 A.M. speech call time, although I was home at 9:00 A.M. My texts were apologetic, especially to Duffy. I took a nap as the responses came pouring in. Everyone seemed to be in mourning, and all said they loved me and still had my back one hundred percent.

Later that evening, I took a deep breath and called Anna. She answered with her characteristic cheery voice despite being eight hours ahead. "Hey, babe! What's up? How was your day?" she greeted me. Heart pounding, I punctured her bright mood. I finished the story with "I'm okay. No one was injured, but it'll be on my record." I needed her to know exactly how much I'd endangered my future.

She responded with love and concern. She asked if everything really was okay, if I wanted to talk to somebody, if I needed anything, how I was feeling. "I'm good. Just a dumb mistake. I'll be all right," I said, feeling utterly hollow. I spent the rest of the day in recluse mode.

The next morning, I sprang into action. After conferring with mentors, I alerted the local press myself. The reporter I called thought it was some cruel joke and refused to believe me, which made the conversation even harder, as I had to convince him that it was, indeed, true. True Son was slated to begin a press run the next week, and producers were adamant that I confront the DUI with a live, in-person interview. I was nervous as hell as I stepped onto the set to speak with Melissa Harris-Perry. Under the intensity of the national television lights, I revealed my biggest mistake to the world and meant every word of my apology. I focused not on the details, but the outcome: "I am deeply sorry," I said, looking at both Melissa Harris-Perry and directly into the camera. "It was a terrible decision. I am getting help to ensure that this never happens again."

In the following weeks, I enrolled in mandatory DUI training and also sought counsel from my pastor, Glenn Shields. We spent months working through whether this DUI and my binge-drinking habits were a sign that the demands put on me by my work were too much or were a cry for help. Alcoholism, I had to acknowledge, was an inherited danger for me: I remembered the childhood vow I had made to never drink after seeing my grandfather, Papa, covered in blood multiple times from drunken falls. He had paid for our private school elementary education, but it was hearing him talk himself through the night with a bottle in his hands night after night that formed the lasting impression I had of him.

Eventually, I learned that he sought in drinking relief from his PTSD from serving in Vietnam. My pastor and I developed accountability mechanisms to help break the cycle of alcohol dependency.

I also had to confront my pride in not making mistakes. When other people messed up, I was quick to feel for them, to forgive them, but it was often from a place of pity. I put a lot of pressure on myself to get everything right the first time, partly because of where and how I grew up. In my resentment of both my father's and my grandfather's conditions, I was shielded from the reality that I, too, was fallible. My DUI forced me to be realistic about my own behavior and to extend grace to others, to realize that personal shortcomings aren't simply a matter of will or discipline, but rooted in generational issues, and even biology. It was humbling for me to see how one mistake made in a split second could endanger everything I'd worked for. We're all just one bad choice away from ruin. We're all human.

I was arrested on Saturday. There was a council meeting on Tuesday. Heading into that meeting, I spent the day fasting and praying because I knew it was going to be brutal. I didn't ask anyone to attend on my behalf, thinking I needed to face the heat by myself. My mom insisted on coming anyway: "I don't want you to be by yourself."

The most difficult part of city council meetings is the public comment portion, when members of the public fill out a blue card and are allowed three minutes to address the council about anything on their mind. Occasionally, a constituent would raise a legitimate issue, but we got a lot of people who just enjoyed seeing themselves on the public access station or who wanted to make provocative comments for shock value. Under Mayor Silva, public comment was used to ridicule those of us on council who did not agree with him, as he stacked the comments with allies. I had been targeted before, but I expected this time to be exceptionally rough. Now Silva had actual ammunition: the "Golden Child," as he often would refer to me disparagingly, had committed a crime.

When that day's public comment started, Mayor Silva looked a little gleeful. I glanced at his hand: the city clerk announced that fifty cards had been submitted. I said a silent prayer as I prepared myself for fifty different people pouring salt on my wound.

A twelve-year-old student from the book club, dressed in a suit, stepped up to the microphone. "Councilman Tubbs,

I wear suits because you wear suits and I look up to you. I know you made a mistake. It hurts my heart, but you can't give up, please. Promise you won't give up."

As it turned out, forty-seven of the fifty commenters were people there to support me. Many of them were distraught, crying, but not accusatory. Local leaders of community organizations came forward: Ms. Bivens, former deputy city manager and my NAACP youth advisor, looked directly at me as she stood at the dais and said, "We don't care what other people are saying, we don't want you to step down. We need you to step up. You're young, made a mistake. It's not acceptable. We'll deal with that, but this is not the time to cower and quake. This is time to really stand up."

I almost cried on the dais. It was too much.

I mouthed apologies to my colleagues as it became clear that the entirety of public comments would be focused on me. A familiar critic who attended every council meeting and was close with the mayor, was the one most thrown off. By the time he approached the mic, the mood in the room was so changed that he said only: "I can't even say what I was going to say," and walked off.

Words of wisdom from my pastor rung in my head: "When the Lord takes pleasure in anyone's way, he causes their enemies to make peace with them."

Months later, during the campaign for mayor, another critic of mine divulged to the press that Mayor Silva had personally asked her and others to come to the council meeting that day. If they gave me hell, he'd promised, he would give them more than their allotted three minutes to do it.

After completing my court-appointed DUI courses, I was so used to thinking about my mistake as a learning opportunity that I decided to talk to students directly about it. I started at Langston Hughes, where I looked at former colleagues, students, and mentees in the eye and told them:

"You're human, so sometimes you'll make choices you shouldn't make, and this is what you do: You own it. You say, 'I'm sorry, I was wrong.' You don't make excuses. 'I'm sorry. I was wrong.' You get help. You make sure it doesn't happen again and you forgive yourself. You forgive other people. You use your mistakes as a chance to help others."

The whole incident reminded me that not only did I love Stockton but my city also loved me, not just for what I did as a councilmember but for who I was. At my lowest moment, my hometown showed me mercy, love, and grace. I realized, newly, the magnitude of what I had been given. Not in terms of influence or authority, but of something far more valuable and precious: trust. People actually trusted me, believed in me, felt hope about my leadership. Given my age and the speed at which everything had happened for me, I had not truly understood the importance of the stewardship I held. I wouldn't make the same mistake again.

At twenty-four years old, my dad and so many like him were not given a second chance. At twenty-four years old, I was. It made real to me the adage of lawyer Bryan Stevenson: We are all more than the worst thing we have ever done. In a sense, the DUI caused me to develop another form of survivor's guilt, the guilt of being given the chance to atone and try again. Ever since then, this guilt has driven me to orient my work to answer the question, "What if we lived in a society that actually gave people the opportunity for redemption?"

We are all more than the worst things we've done.

A journalist from *The Stockton Record* contacted me and

asked me for a list of all my accomplishments on the city council over the past two and a half years. His article, imploring that I stay in city government, was headlined: "Heavy Hitter Isn't Out with One Strike."

In the third of my four years on the city council, I began to think about what I wanted to do next. There was an opening on the County Board of Supervisors, which was an attractive political position: full-time with full-time pay, plus less stress and scrutiny than my current role. As supervisor, I would continue to represent my council district and be in control of all the services my constituents needed, from healthcare to education to probation to workforce training. San Joaquin County had never had a Black supervisor. A poll was conducted and found that I was twenty to twenty-five points ahead of anyone else who might run.

It was the next logical step. I brought Nicholas Hatten on again to serve as my campaign manager and announced that I would be running for county supervisor.

Instead of excitement about entering a race as the front runner, though, I felt on edge. The mayoral race was shaping up with the incumbent and two sitting county supervisors leading the pack, and I couldn't stop thinking about it. Nothing about the idea of me running for mayor made sense: I was young, twenty-five years old. I'd just received a DUI. The mayor is the face of the city, and Stockton had never had a Black mayor. And it was risky: my city council seat was up at the same time, so if I lost the race for mayor, I'd also lose my council seat. I wouldn't be an elected official anymore. The county supervisor position paid even more. And yet the thought of running for mayor continued to burn in the back of my mind. It would be the road less taken, but my subconscious was telling me that it would make all the difference.

One of my mentors, Steve Bestolarides, was running for mayor. He had insisted we make a deal back in 2013 that if he ran, I wouldn't run. Back then I had just gotten on the council, so it would have never occurred to me to run for mayor. *I ain't tryin to be nobody's mayor,* I'd thought. But he's a smart man. He could see the future when I couldn't. And he wasn't the only one: when I had the internship at the White House back in the fall of 2010, my boss there had heard me speak about Stockton and predicted that I'd be running for mayor in 2016. At the time, I'd said: "No way. 2024, maybe, but not 2016." But his prediction stuck with me.

To deal with my conflicting feelings about which office to run for, as I do with every major decision, I prayed about it. Prayer for me is usually on the go and not terribly long, but enough to get some perspective. Sometimes I'm a little demanding, I'll admit. This particular prayer was at lunch and ended with: *I don't want to do anything that's outside of Your will, as that has served me well thus far. If you want me to run for mayor, then Steve Bestolarides has to drop out the race.*

The next day, I had lunch with Kathy Miller, a former councilmember colleague of mine who had just become county supervisor. We were sizing up the local political field when she mentioned that a rumor was going around: Steve was thinking about dropping out of the mayoral race. My heart raced, with more fear than excitement.

"What? Why's he dropping out?" Steve had raised the most money. He had all the endorsements. But he decided to pursue the county assessor position, as the hours and the pay made more sense for his family than serving as the mayor.

"When did you hear about this?"

"At lunch yesterday."

The look on my face made Kathy lean forward in concern. "Are you okay?"

"Oh yeah, I'm fine."

Reassured that I wasn't unwell, she carried on: "If this is actually true, it'll be great! You'll be a supervisor. Hopefully, Elbert Holman will consider running for mayor . . ." Elbert was an older Black gentleman who was the longest serving member of the city council and had also served as a sheriff and head of investigations for the district attorney's office. An august contender.

After lunch, I just sat in my car, struck with wonder. If what Kathy had shared was true, then around the same time I made my vow to run for mayor if Steve dropped out of the race, Steve began to consider dropping out of the race. It was literally the sign I'd asked for, even if it defied logic.

The following week, I was at an event with the police chief. He pulled me aside.

"Councilman Tubbs, I shouldn't do this. I'm not really supposed to get into politics. But you know how hard I work. I would really appreciate if you considered running for mayor."

I had huge respect for him, and I *did* know how hard he worked. Since I'd been on the council, he and I had worked closely together, creating the Office of Violence Prevention and mandating body cameras. I found Chief Jones to be understated yet innovative, and incredibly empathetic. I would routinely chide him, saying, "You are way too nice to be someone's police chief!" But he was tough on process, not people. He routinely implored the community to invest in other anti-poverty assets, including social workers or therapists, to make his job easier. As the Black Lives Matter movement was forming nationally, he'd signed the city up for President Obama's National Trust Initiative and started use-of-force listening tours and racial-reconciliation sessions. We implemented implicit bias training for all of our officers. And this was back in 2015!

All this to say: Chief Jones was, and is, a universally beloved figure in the Stockton community. As a councilmember, I was keenly aware of the importance of the mayor–police chief relationship. I began thinking of the possibilities of showing that a vision for safety beyond law enforcement was possible—and that it could be done with a middle-aged white police chief and a millennial Black mayor working side by side.

That very same week, Jane Butterfield, the head of the business council and part of Old Stockton, with whom I had built an unlikely friendship, sat me down and said, "You should run for Mayor." We were co-chairs of Measure A and B, the tax measure that gave the city resources to hire more officers, exit bankruptcy, and fund the Office of Violence Prevention. Jane reminded me of my three moms and Jan Barker: she was fierce, opinionated, and got things done. I was nervous about telling her my new political ambitions, as I wasn't sure if I would have her support. Relief flooded over me as I realized she had come to the same conclusion.

At twenty-five years old, I had garnered the trust of a business heavyweight and our police chief.

In my work as a councilmember, I realized, I had been assembling the type of coalition needed to not only win but to govern a city as diverse as Stockton. I had the support of many of the grassroots groups and activists, community-based organizations, law enforcement, and the business community. At this point it seemed like the path to run for mayor was being cleared by forces larger than myself.

I thought about my experiences in the classroom. I knew I would miss the relationships I had built with my students. I had learned so much about the hopes and aspirations of their families and neighborhoods, intel that made me a more relevant politician, in my opinion. Still, I knew I wasn't able to make change at scale in my classroom; I needed to devote all of my time to changing the environment my students came from so that they could focus in the classroom and do their best.

What I could do, as I prepared to transition to full-time political work, was ensure that the school board had the kind of leadership that would truly fight to improve education in Stockton. I called Lange. We brainstormed great candidates for school board members, but came up short. I looked to Lange.

"If you're not going to run, who will?" I said.

Lange declined. He loved the work he was doing as a teacher and as a parent organizer for the Stockton Schools Initiative, an organization we had cofounded. He was also cognizant of the fact that he had gone to school outside the Stockton Unified School District and felt strongly that an alum of the district should run for the seat. I spent the next couple of days pleading with him, reminding him of the frustrations of the parents he worked with, who weren't able to get the district to meet with them, or listen to their commonsense concerns about their kids' education. I told him that his Harvard education and Stockton upbringing had prepared him for the opportunity to govern. Eventually, he relented. He also felt it was important for the board and for students to have Filipino and LGBT representation, which he could provide.

I was elated. I was confident Lange would elevate the board, but I also loved that one of my best friends and I would be on the same ballot.

Meanwhile, I decided that I was going to run for mayor.

I only faced one more complication: my fellow councilmember, Elbert Holman. I was not going to run against him. I had great respect for him, and I knew he really wanted to be mayor and deserved it. He had deep roots in Stockton, and had never left. His dad had been a janitor at city hall and would walk him into the chambers and tell him that he could be up there one day. Elbert attended Edison High School and UOP. Beginning in the early 1970s, he had served as the deputy sheriff, then as a detective and sergeant. After twenty years in the sheriff's department, he was appointed as an investigator for the sheriff's department and the district attorney's office. He grew up in a time when, as a Black man, he wasn't allowed north of Harding Way, a dividing line that separated the northern part of the city from downtown and South and East Stockton. On the council, he represented the northernmost part of the city. Now in his late sixties, he liked to joke that he had shoes older than me.

I was nervous about the conversation and stalled on reaching out. Elbert called me himself and got straight to the point. "Listen, councilman. People are pressuring me. Let's do this: you make your decision first. If you want to run for mayor, I won't run. I defer to you."

It absolutely should have been the other way around. He had been on the council for eight years and helped to get the city out of bankruptcy. He had a lifetime of service to the city. I had the next forty years to run for mayor. But he was pragmatic enough for the both of us, saying: "I would love to be mayor, but you bring a hope and excitement that this city needs. I would be good as mayor, but you would be best."

I told him I needed a couple days to think about it, although in my heart I knew what I was going to do. On September fifth, I made my announcement that I was no longer running for board of supervisors, but instead running to be mayor of Stockton. I promised myself that if I got elected, Elbert was going to be the vice-mayor. I had always been impressed with his work and integrity, but his humility blew me away.

Before the mayoral campaign was at full throttle, I surprised myself and made the trek to Folsom State Prison. Once or twice a year since serving as a councilmember, I was invited to Soledad State Prison and others to meet with the inmates, but this trip was plainly personal. I didn't announce my plans ahead of time, deciding to surprise my father with a visit.

Entering the visiting room still felt as awkward to me as it had more than a decade ago. I could not help but notice that I was the only man in the room who wasn't a guard or an inmate: all the other visitors were women and children. I saw a couple of boys who looked like me when I was their age, their happiness to see their father overshadowed by the absence they had to live with day to day.

My father smiled when I walked in, but didn't appear too surprised. I marveled at how he looked similar to my memory of him from when I saw him at age twelve, just more grizzled, hardened.

We played cards and kept the conversation mostly superficial, but I couldn't help notice ways in which we are similar, little mannerisms, the fact that everyone in the visitors' room knew him and called out his name: "Mike! Mike!" He had started mentoring some of the younger guys, newer arrivals, trying to give them all his hard-won insights about surviving inside and not getting sent back once they got out. He said his goal in life was to make me proud of him the way he was proud of me.

There was a song out called "Down in the DM" by Yo Gotti that had been getting a lot of play, and while we were playing cards, we both started singing the song at the exact same time, without any conversation beforehand. It was funny and tragic at the same time.

As I left, I felt such a heaviness, a mourning for all that had been lost. I played J. Cole's song "Breakdown" in the car, and the tears flowed freely. I cried for my father in a way that I had never cried before. There were a lot of tears, twenty-six years in the making, tears I had never shed for him as a kid, so determined had I been to be the rose that grew from concrete. I felt the weight of it all, the second chance even I, his son, had denied him for so long. J. Cole sang in the background:

> Just seen my father for the first time in a minute,
> And when I say a minute I mean years, man
> Damn, a whale could have swam in them tears fam

The tears were cathartic. After our last visit, I had resolved to prove him wrong about my future. This time I resolved to do the work necessary to change the structures and the system of Stockton so that little boys are able to know their fathers.

The mayoral primary featured several Stockton personalities and sitting elected officials. There was no love lost between the incumbent, Mayor Silva, and me. Supervisor

Carlos Villapudua was also a formidable opponent, and was actually the supervisor whose seat I was originally running to replace. Having held his former position for eight years (and now termed out), he was the highest ranking Latino male elected official in a city that is 40 percent Latino. We had similar bases of support in South Stockton. He was well-liked, someone to get a beer with, which made him a challenge. But I felt he was less of a visionary and more of a man who needed a new job.

There were another five people running, making eight total, but the three of us were considered the leading candidates.

Two weeks before Get Out the Vote weekend during the primary, Mayor Silva called me. We had never talked on the phone before, as I preferred to text or not talk to him at all, so I knew something was up.

"Hey, Tubbs, I want you to know I'm not going to go negative on you. Let's make a truce. No negative campaigning."

I went straight to my campaign staff. "Get ready for negative attacks."

"Why?"

"Anthony just called me and proposed a truce. It's not going to come from him. But he made a deal with someone. He's juvenile."

In observing Mayor Silva as a councilmember, I had noticed a pattern to his moves. He thought he was cunning, while blatantly telegraphing his moves. Whenever he did something out of the ordinary, especially something that seemed kind, I learned to expect the opposite. Time and again, he would compliment councilmembers out of the blue right before our meetings, only to slam them in public. I figured if he was calling, he and Carlos had spoken about getting me out of the primary. It made sense: Carlos and he had been political allies before the race and were rumored to be sharing the same political consultant, Allen Sawyer.

A week or so later, I was at the gym, which is not my favorite place to be. I wish I was more athletic and in shape, but then I don't enjoy working out . . . it's a struggle. Running is, at least, efficient exercise, so there I was on the treadmill, venting my campaign anxiety and boosting my spirits with gospel music. "The Battle Is the Lord's" by Yolanda Adams filled my ears, my feet pounding out the song's rhythm on the belt.

I looked up, and my DUI mug shot was on the screen. Not just on one screen—all the screens. Every TV in the place. A week before the election. My opponent had bought commercials during Memorial Day weekend on Oxygen, CNN, ESPN . . . every channel at the gym was showing the same ad.

After my mug shot there was a line of text: "Tubbs takes instruction from ex-felons."

I wanted to disappear. I scanned the gym to see if anyone recognized me as I hightailed it out of there.

Allegedly, Silva had made a deal with Carlos Villapudua, who had raised more money than the dubiously popular incumbent. Carlos paid for the attack ads in an attempt to make sure that he and Mayor Silva made it out of the primary and advanced to the November runoff.

Despite the unholy alliance, I won a plurality with 34 percent of the vote. Mayor Silva won 25 percent, and Carlos 23 percent. Ironically for him, if Carlos had run attack ads on Silva instead of on me, he would have almost certainly made it to second place rather than third place, because statistically attack ads generally knock people down 2 to 3 percent. That would have pitted him against me in the runoff.

Choices have consequences.

The negativity continued during the general election run-off, with Silva employing Trump-like lying and mudslinging before the presidency of Donald Trump. He played on all the racist tropes: "Tubbs has never had a job. He listens to criminals. He wants to spend all the taxpayer dollars." He doctored photos to show me wearing a diaper, with the creative slogan, "Do you want a baby running your city?" High school student council campaigns had more decorum.

During one of our debates, Silva called himself the city's first Black mayor. This was at a debate hosted by the NAACP and Black Women Organized for Political Action. I made it a point to say that representation matters, and that it was sad and surprising that, in 150 years, Stockton had never seen a Black mayor. We were going to change that in this election, I said.

Silva, who is ethnically Portuguese, chimed in: "With all due respect, I might be the first African American mayor the city's ever had."

I was incensed but stayed focused. "Clearly, he's not Black," I said. "But beyond that, look at his policies. His policies have been harmful to Black people." I brought up a "sagging ordinance" he'd proposed, in which law enforcement could police young men about how they wore their pants, as if they had nothing better (and less racially charged) to do. (Luckily, the entire council and the police chief had disagreed with that proposal.)

After the debate, I was upset to see that most Black leaders acted like Silva's lie was no big deal. In a statement to the press, he defended the claim by explaining that he had been mentoring several African American youths in South and East Stockton, and that each summer he hired African American lifeguards. He then doubled down to say that I *wasn't* Black, because I went to Stanford: that he was the true representative of the Black community in Stockton.

It was a Trumpian tactic, I would reflect later: standing by a position so ridiculous that most people just ignored it.

Then there were his actual crimes. In August 2016 it came out that the FBI was investigating Silva. An article in *The New York Times* summarized it:

> First, the residents of Stockton, Calif., learned that their mayor was the owner of a stolen gun linked to a homicide. Days later, he was arrested at a camp he runs for disadvantaged youths, accused of secretly recording teenagers playing strip poker, providing alcohol to minors and endangering children there a year earlier.

Further scrutiny revealed earlier police reports on Silva's recording girls using the restroom and changing clothes, and a nineteen-year-old woman's accusation of sexual battery. None of those reports had led to criminal charges, conveniently. I took no joy in these revelations, just great sadness. How could someone so depraved win elections as both school board president and mayor?

After that, it didn't matter how low my opponent struck. We knew the election was ours to lose.

In October, I reached out to President Obama's political director on Twitter in a direct message. I had kept in touch with people in the White House since my internship and wanted to give him an update on my campaign with the small hope that the president would decide to endorse it.

On October 31, 2016, I received an email from the White House saying they were considering endorsing me. That was six years to the day after my cousin Donnell had been murdered, on Halloween night 2010, while I was interning in the White House.

I sent the White House everything they asked for—a prospectus of the race and my policy platform—and secured the endorsement of President Obama on November 1, 2016. He didn't call me or anything; I just received a confirmation email from his people. Still, it was a big deal, and the response to my announcing the news on social media was overwhelming. People were surprised, but moved, that Obama cared about Stockton. And I couldn't help thinking about how I had been an intern just six years earlier.

On November 8, 2016, I received 70 percent of the vote to become mayor of Stockton. At twenty-six years old, four years out of college, eight years out of high school, I was the youngest person in the United States ever to be elected mayor of a city with a population of more than 100,000. And I was Stockton's first Black mayor.

I made Elbert Holman my vice-mayor, as I'd promised I would. That same night, Lange was elected the youngest member of Stockton's school board, the first out gay man to win office in the San Joaquin Valley. The night was one of great hope for the city, even as the news broke that the country had taken a huge step backward with the election of Donald Trump.

I refused to let Trump's victory that same night overshadow

what we had accomplished together. In fact, it made me believe only more fervently that Stockton was poised to be an example to the nation, an example of progress even when perfection seemed distant. At my swearing-in I said:

"During the past four years, I've met countless people both here and nationally who are disillusioned with government. People who believe government far too often gets in the way, is not responsive to citizens, does not care about their day-to-day realities, and that those who are making decisions on their behalf don't have their best interests at heart. These beliefs have given rise to a lack of faith in the ability of government to do anything well. Tonight represents a rejection of that notion, a reinvention if you will, and an invitation to believe again, Stockton.

"To believe not just in me, but in we."

These were the truths behind my speech: that Stockton was a place where my grandmother, my aunt, and my mother could work hard their whole lives yet still face housing insecurity, job insecurity, lack of adequate healthcare, and lack of access to healthy food. That in Stockton, young Black men like my father, my cousin Donnell, and myself are at constant risk of bodily harm and despair. And that my city's poverty, violence, and educational lapses are part of larger systems in this country that have worked to the advantage of a few people, while disadvantaging the rest.

Something is wrong, I knew as I stood on that podium, when one in two Americans can't afford a single four-hundred-dollar emergency without it rendering them homeless or otherwise ruining their lives. Something is wrong when wages have increased only 6 percent between 1979 and 2013. Something is wrong when people working two and three jobs can't pay for necessities like rent, electricity, healthcare, or childcare.

These structures we inherit weren't acts of God but acts of men and women. They were policy choices, made by elected politicians. That meant we had the capacity to change them.

I concluded my speech:

"With these choices, we are poised to become a model of urban renewal. A model of unity, not division, a model of hope and not fear, a model of action and not apathy, a model of problem solving and not pettiness, a model of bridges and not walls, a model of the benefits of diversity, a community of opportunity and hope.

"Stockton, I am more resolute than ever in my belief that our city's best days are ahead. I say this because I know you and I know us.

"In the words of the prophet Isaiah, 'Forget the former things; do not dwell on the past. See, I am doing a new thing! Now it springs up; do you not perceive it? I am making a way in the wilderness and streams in the wasteland.'"

After my DUI, the people of Stockton gifted me a second chance. I would never forget that. I would use it. The work I had already begun to do (open up health clinics, close liquor stores, and reform the police department) was a good foundation to build on. My next task was to make sure I brought everything I had—all of my experiences, all of my childhood, and all of my neighbors, too—into the mayor's office with me.

14

JERICHO ROAD

My mothers at first refused to entertain the notion that Anna and I would be living together before we were married. I found this a little rich, given that me; my brother, Dre; and my cousins Shaleeka and Scharlyce, all born out of wedlock, were proof that my moms didn't quite follow every biblical precept. To be fair, I had to get used to the idea of Anna moving in, too. But she was persuasive.

"Mike, if we're going to eventually get married, we are going to have to live with each other. We should figure out what that's like now," she reasoned. I liked that long view. So, after she completed her master's degree at Cambridge University in the United Kingdom, she moved in with me in South Stockton.

The initial adjustment was rough. Aside from my senior year in college, we had been in a long-distance relationship for five years. Now we had to break down the compartmentalization of our lives. Introducing Anna into my political events was particularly awkward: people fumbled over how to refer to her and often excluded her from conversations about my future, clearly assuming we weren't serious enough that she would be there. More than once I heard her called my "trophy girlfriend."

Anna was nobody's trophy, of course—and she was very serious. She found a job teaching social studies at Langston Hughes Academy, and over the course of 2016 made me aware of just how much her family, friends, *my* family, and others were asking her when we were going to get married or why weren't we married yet. (No one ever asked me!) Although laser-focused on the campaign, I had made it one of my New Year's resolutions to propose and was already saving up for a ring. I worked with a jewelry designer friend to find the perfect one and swallowed the entire-month's-paycheck price tag. I thought of proposing on election night, but didn't want our engagement to be connected to politics. I decided that I would propose after the election but before the new year—a year I planned to start as a fiancé and as mayor.

By late summer, I had the ring in my possession, unbeknownst to Anna. The only hitch: Anna hates not knowing things.

In the middle of an October night, three weeks before the election, she shook me awake. I jumped from REM sleep, expecting to hear some terrible news or to have to confront an intruder.

"You're never going to propose!"

"What are you talking about?" I rubbed the sleep from my eyes and tried to focus on her.

"I'm just going to have to propose, because you'll never do it."

The ring was literally hidden underneath the bed. I was annoyed at first by her lack of faith in me, but then I smiled. I was going to propose to someone who knew what she wanted and left nothing to chance, which weren't terrible traits to have in a life partner.

To throw her off the scent, I told her that I planned to propose on Valentine's Day and that she had ruined my grand surprise. I did my best to make her feel guilty for thinking that I didn't even have a plan. She replied with an, "Oh. Okay," rolled over, and went to sleep again.

I made a mental note that I did actually need to make a proposal plan.

Soon afterward, Lange, daydreaming about post-campaign life, found cheap tickets to Cartagena, Colombia, and said we had to go there after the election. "Trump might actually get elected," he joked, "and we are going to want to leave the country at least for a little bit." I had never been to Cartagena and neither had Anna, so we planned a double-date vacation with Lange and his partner. I realized that the trip was also an ideal proposal setting: beautiful and totally separate from politics. Lange thought it was a great idea, and in true Lange fashion helped me to plan a perfect surprise for Anna.

We arranged a private walking tour of Cartagena that took us through the city's history. The colonial-era architecture is colorful and charming, but our guide reminded us that the prosperity of the city was built on the theft of the indigenous people's gold and the labor of enslaved Africans. We walked through the Plaza de los Coches, the square inside the city gates where a plaque informs you that more than one million slaves were sold there. Anna and I both remarked at Cartagena's embrace of its dark history: the city speaks the truth about its past atrocities as a vow to never repeat them.

The proposal was to happen at sunset on the roof of the church of San Pedro Claver. It was a beautiful spot, set high on a point, surrounded by views of the water. As a bonus, it turned out that the church and monastery were named after Father Pedro Claver, known in his day as "the apostle of the Negroes." He was a Spanish priest and abolitionist who focused his ministry on the most marginalized members of Colombian society. I didn't realize the history at the time I made my plans. But it fit.

We'd arranged for a professional photographer to capture the moment, so that morning Lange had tried his best to persuade Anna to wear a dress, or anything more elegant than athletic wear and sneakers. He'd gone so far as to say she wouldn't be allowed in the churches we planned to visit if she was wearing pants.

"How antiquated is that?!" she practically snorted. "Then I won't go in."

"Do you like how your hair looks like that?" Lange persisted as she put her hair back in a French braid.

"What is wrong with you?!" she said.

Asked for my opinion, I responded with a Drake lyric: "Sweatpants, hair tie, chilling with no makeup on, that's when you're the prettiest, I hope that you don't take that wrong."

All day I rushed everyone along, worried we'd be late for the finale.

"Since when do you care about us being on time to things?" Anna exclaimed.

As it turned out, we had time to kill before sunset, so our guide took us into the Museo de la Esmeralda, one of the city's many emerald stores. According to the "museum," the gem was the favorite stone of Cleopatra and Beyoncé.

"I didn't realize how much I loved emeralds!" Anna was

giddy, practically jumping up and down. "When you propose, I want my ring to have emeralds, Michael!"

I looked at Lange in panic. We exchanged whispers: mine hysterical, his reassuring.

"Lange, I have to get her a ring from here. You heard her! She just said she wants emeralds, Lange!"

"Tubbs, calm down. She doesn't want an emerald ring."

"But she just *said*—!"

Then it was almost sunset. To reach the church we had to climb a set of narrow stairs and pass through a sort of cave.

"Are you okay?" Anna asked me, knowing I'm claustrophobic and don't like heights.

"I'm fine. Just keep walking, please." I had to focus on quelling my anxiety.

We reached the roof of the church, which was as spectacular as promised, with views of the city all around. The sun was at the horizon. Our guide, Lange, and Lange's partner all melted into the background.

"Anna, I love you so much."

I got down on one knee.

"Wait, what?"

"Will you marry me?"

"What? Here? Now?" She started crying.

After what seemed like forever, she said yes.

I am still the luckiest man in the world.

My four years on the city council had been a good introduction to local government, but nothing prepared me for the emotional and mental rigors of being the mayor of a major American city. As a councilmember, I could afford to be narrow in focus; as mayor, people wanted my take even on issues over which I had no formal authority. I could also fly below the radar as a councilmember, where as mayor there was nowhere to hide. I was (am) astounded by how much people cared about what I did outside of work—where I worked out (on the very rare occasions), where Anna and I chose to eat on a weekend, my physical appearance, what music I listened to, what I tweeted. Couple that with the job of actual governing, and it was hard not to feel quickly overwhelmed.

The pressure was on. Stockton was home.

I spent my first 100 days thinking through the metrics I would use to determine success. How could I ensure that it mattered that I was mayor, that government would change because there was someone different at the policy-making table? Historically, the halls of power have been restricted to those who fit select demographics. As a first-generation college student, a Black male, and the child of a teenage mother and incarcerated father, I was keenly aware that I didn't fit the image most people had of a political leader. It was people from backgrounds like mine, however, who tended to be most adversely affected by policy and who needed the government to work for them the most. Far too often, I knew, leaders' life experiences become a moat or wall between them and their constituents, as they marginalize others' lived realities that are unlike their own. I wanted to use my experiences as a bridge.

I resolved early on to maximize time and resources during my term by focusing on long-term structural issues, addressing underlying causes rather than just their day-to-day effects. This orientation often caused tension with the daily realities and ceremonial functions of the job, but I was determined to move the needle. My governing philosophy was the culmination of personal experience, my time at Stanford, and observations as a councilmember. But no foundation was more important, as usual, than the biblical wisdom of my nana.

The Good Samaritan parable (Luke, chapter 10) was often on my mind:

> ²⁹ But he wanted to justify himself, so he asked Jesus, "And who is my neighbor?"
>
> ³⁰ In reply Jesus said: "A man was going down from Jerusalem to Jericho, when he was attacked by robbers. They stripped him of his clothes, beat him and went away, leaving him half dead. ³¹ A priest happened to be going down the same road, and when he saw the man, he passed by on the other side. ³² So too, a Levite, when he came to the place and saw him, passed by on the other side. ³³ But a Samaritan, as he traveled, came where the man was; and when he saw him, he took pity on him. ³⁴ He went to him and bandaged his wounds, pouring on oil and wine. Then he put the man on his own donkey, brought him to an inn and took care of him. ³⁵ The next day he took out two denarii and gave them to the innkeeper. 'Look after him,' he said, 'and when I return, I will reimburse you for any extra expense you may have.'
>
> ³⁶ "Which of these three do you think was a neighbor to the man who fell into the hands of robbers?"
>
> ³⁷ The expert in the law replied, "The one who had mercy on him."
>
> Jesus told him, "Go and do likewise."

In my career thus far, I had sought to be like the Good Samaritan by addressing my neighbors' immediate needs. I created programs like the Phoenix Scholars and the Summer Success and Leadership Academy to give my students access to opportunities, and as a councilmember I focused on concrete fixes like adding a health clinic and building a bank in South Stockton.

When I became mayor, however, the cyclical nature of Stockton's problems—poverty, lack of opportunity, poor education—challenged me to understand that being a Good Samaritan was necessary, but not sufficient to produce the change my community deserved. Yes, as mayor I had to ensure that the city understood we were responsible for our neighbors. But values like charity and empathy alone weren't going to address the reasons we needed Good Samaritans in the first place.

The road featured in the parable, where the man is left for dead, was literally structured for violence. Narrow and meandering, with ample hiding places, it was so conducive for ambushing that it was nicknamed the Bloody Pass. A man on the side of that road wasn't abnormal. Violence was a predictable outcome of travel, given the structure of the road to Jericho. It was working according to design.

After taking the man to the inn and dealing with his immediate needs, the Good Samaritan might have gone back to figure out how to prevent the same fate from happening to others. If he had, he might have realized that, despite his heroism, people were going to keep getting hurt unless the underlying conditions of the road itself were changed. What could be done, the most determined Samaritan might have asked, to change the structure of the road?

This question—How can we change the road?—became

the guiding force behind all my work as mayor of the City of Stockton.

At the heart of Stockton's struggles is poverty. It is grinding and endemic and affects everything, from the low rates of educational attainment, to the historically anemic economic development, to the high rates of crime and violence. It intersects with sexism and racism, as women—most often Black women—are left to bear alone the burden of households whose men are incarcerated, formerly incarcerated, or dead before their time. If we were going to fix Stockton's road, addressing poverty had to be part of the answer.

During my first 100 days as mayor, I convened my team of policy fellows, led by a brilliant recent Stanford graduate, Patrick Cirenza, to research the most direct interventions to combat poverty. I told them that when the status quo is this untenable, the greatest risk would be to do nothing. Armed with the confidence to be bold, they came back with a radically simple solution: give people money.

The idea took me back to Dr. King's last book, which I had read during college: *Where Do We Go from Here: Chaos or Community?* In it I discovered King's dream of economic dignity for all Americans. At eighteen, I highlighted the words: "I am now convinced that the simplest approach will prove to be the most effective—the solution to poverty is to abolish it directly by a now widely discussed measure: the guaranteed income." King's proposal struck me on a visceral level. I had watched my family struggle to make ends meet all my life. I saw my mom work constantly and fight against debt, all while being stressed about how close we were to disaster. What if she'd had a financial cushion, any at all?

My team pointed to work being done in other countries at the time, including Canada and Kenya. They also found that President Nixon had researched guaranteed income programs. I knew about Dr. King's views, but had no idea about this. "Nixon?" I asked, incredulous. Back then, apparently, the Republican president had been as on board as the idea's Democratic sponsors. The only difference between the Democrats' plan for a basic income and Nixon's was that Nixon wanted to impose work requirements. Either way, every adult American citizen would have gotten a check.

Although I loved the concept of guaranteed income, I was initially hesitant to take such an untested swing in my first year as mayor. I pushed my team to find me the results of an American experiment with the concept and help me understand the politics of why it didn't pass. They responded with the results of the study from the U.S. Office of Economic Opportunity. The researchers found that, with the guaranteed income, some people's unemployment spells lasted longer—workers had more agency and bargaining power and could secure jobs with better pay and hours that treated them with dignity. The researchers also found that because women were able to be more financially independent, divorce rates increased as they had the financial freedom to walk away from abusive or dead-end marriages.

The findings led to the policy's death in Congress. To me, however, this data sounded great. I began thinking about how we could finance such a program. Given the political realities of Stockton and our resources—we had only recently exited bankruptcy—I knew it would be difficult to convince my colleagues to test this idea. Maybe we could use some of the newly legalized cannabis revenue to fund a trial? I told my team to put guaranteed income on the back burner until term two.

No one outside of our office knew we were even researching the idea of a guaranteed income when, at a tech industry conference on the future of work, a woman I had met previously as part of Obama World, Natalie Foster, told me that her organization was looking for cities to pilot a UBI program. The Economic Security Project was funded and co-chaired by a co-founder of Facebook, Chris Hughes, who thought a basic income could be a powerful tool for solving economic insecurity. I told Natalie about our existing taskforce on the idea, and we walked away from the conference agreeing to explore a collaboration.

We spent a year in design mode, led by the effective (and even younger than me!) program director Sukhi Samra, working alongside the community and starting with the question: "What would five hundred dollars mean to you?" People's answers were profound, humbling. I heard some things I expected, alongside so many things I could never have anticipated.

One lady said: "I could get my car fixed, my transmission fixed, which would let me get a stable job. As it is, I'm not able to get stable work because my car is broken."

A mother answered: "Five hundred dollars would help me more in the summer than the winter."

"Why?" we asked her.

"Because in the summer my kids come home from school, so my utility bills go up, my food bill goes up. I get stressed and anxious when they come home. I don't want them to think they can't come home. So that would make me comfortable to know that when they come home, I can afford it."

A small business owner said that he hadn't been able to see

his family in Nashville for four years because he couldn't afford to take a vacation. He would use the money to visit them.

Hearing these answers illustrated to me that the most powerful way to lead my community would be to trust my community, just as I had trusted them to vote for me.

This trust would be tested as we grappled with how to choose participants for the program. I felt strongly that we should stage the pilot in neighborhoods in which we already had other programs running, to layer this effort on top of other programs that were showing success. The board of community representatives we had brought in vehemently disagreed, saying that everyone in the city should have a shot at participation. I ceded to the group's wisdom and we settled on anyone living in zip codes at or below the median income of the city, meaning 76 percent of the city would qualify. This meant that there would be those in the program who made more than the median income and those that made less, folks who were working and folks who were not.

On February 15, 2019, we began the first mayoral-led basic income pilot in this country's history. One hundred thirty families randomly selected from the chosen zip codes began receiving five hundred dollars a month through our pilot program: the Stockton Economic Empowerment Demonstration (SEED) project.

I did not anticipate just how controversial it would be, locally and nationally, to challenge the economic status quo.

In Twitter battles with conservative pundits like Sarah Palin and Chuck Woolery, I fought the all-too-common argument that I could not trust my constituents with the agency to make the best decision for themselves and their families. My opponents held that the issue wasn't with the structure or the road, but with impoverished people themselves, that those left on the side of the road were there because of the choices they made, because they were lazy, because they weren't educated, because they couldn't manage money. In countless interviews I found myself pushing back on tacit racism as othering terms like "they" and "them" were used to describe why a basic income wasn't a good idea, or even an American one. "They don't work hard, they won't work, they'll spend the money on Jordans and drugs and alcohol." Tell that, I thought, to my mom, my aunt, my nana. Tell it to my community.

The real fight, I realized, was not about whether a guaranteed income was the best way to fight poverty, but whether we should fight poverty at all.

Another prevailing notion was the "dignity of work"; the idea that work allows people to feel like they're contributing, to hold their heads high, having earned their keep. The notion troubled me, because I had met so many constituents who worked in undignified conditions: low wages, no paid time off, dangerous work conditions, long hours, and they still couldn't pay the rent. Through the SEED design process, I witnessed how the idea erased the contributions of domestic caregivers and those whose disabilities prevented traditional work—individuals who, too, had dignity.

Attaching the idea of dignity to production is part of the reason we have such a lopsided economy today. Dignity has to be attached to humanity first. No one needs to earn their humanity. By providing an income floor that ensures all people are afforded a baseline standard of living, we could create a humane society that would enable its members to contribute, in traditional work contexts or otherwise, in environments where their dignity is protected.

Six months into the SEED pilot, I spoke with my first recipient, Tomas. He believed that his story would be one that would resonate and provide a clear example of why we were doing the pilot in the first place. In speaking with Tomas, he told me that the extra five hundred dollars had been enough of a cushion for him to interview for a better job. When I asked why it would cost five hundred dollars for an interview, he laughed and responded that he worked hourly with no paid time off and lived paycheck to paycheck with his wife and two kids. Without that extra five hundred dollars per month, he could not have afforded the two unpaid days off he'd needed to pursue the more stable job. He was hired, full-time with benefits, which means that even when the SEED program ends he will continue to be in a much stronger position. He's happier than he's ever been, he says. He and his wife argue less, he gets to spend more time with his kids, and is proud that he is able to pay for things like tutoring, helping to prepare his kids for brighter futures.

Before our conversation concluded I asked him: "What is your response to the people who say that, after this is done, I'm setting you up for failure?"

"With all due respect, Mayor Tubbs, for most people in Stockton our backs are already against a wall. We're as far back as we can go. We can't go back any further. The only way we could go was forward. And this is a good bridge to get us there."

Another target from my term was higher education. Of America's 100 most populous cities, Stockton comes ninety-ninth in adults with a bachelor's degree or higher (only 17 percent). It is the largest city in the state of California and the second-largest metro area in the country without a four-year public educational institution of higher learning. Research bears out that poverty is an indicator of low academic achievement. Although as mayor I had no formal authority over our school system, I resolved to use my position to help our students.

In high school, many of my talented peers declined to apply for selective—or any—colleges because they were worried about finances or didn't have a Carolyn Lawrence to illuminate their process. There also wasn't a culture of expectation, one that assumed every kid had something to offer and should be encouraged to plan for post-graduation. This lack of guidance was doubly frustrating to me because everyone in Stockton had reasons to invest in a more educated community. In meetings with business owners as a councilmember, I heard constant concerns about the quality of our schools from the standpoint of whether they could find an educated-enough workforce.

Now, newly elected Stockton Unified trustees Lange Luntao, Patrick Cirenza, and Sukhi Samra researched the best ways for cities to boost the educational outcomes of their community. We settled on a holistic, "cradle-to-career" plan, supporting kids through all development milestones, anchored by college scholarships for as many kids as we could possibly fund.

As Stanford and my work with the Phoenix Scholars taught me, talent and potential are universal, but resources and opportunity are not. And as growing up in Stockton had taught me, there were no guarantees: you could work really hard in school and still get tripped up, as my friend Frank had when he and his girlfriend had an unplanned pregnancy, or as my student Donovon did when his offer of admission was rescinded because family issues and lack of motivation at the end of high school caused him to fail one of his early college classes at the local community college. For many of my constituents, I knew, hard work didn't guarantee anything but more hard work. You could do everything right and still not receive the promised payoff.

That's why I was adamant that we make a guarantee to our students: a college promise. If they kept working hard for their dreams, I wanted to be able to say that there would be something waiting for them. I also wanted them to know that I saw them. That I knew it was hard, that they were working their asses off to graduate high school and do everything right. That it wasn't easy. That I know some of them were helping to raise their siblings. *You're studying. You're saving money to buy test prep books. You're hungry. Your parents are arguing and crying. If you persist through all that,* I wanted to say, *I got you. We're investing in you, guaranteed. We believe in you and your potential.*

In South Africa, my friend Evan and I had spent a lot of time discussing the opportunity structure of the United States and how education could be the great equalizer. We kept in contact after college, as I did my electoral thing and he became the world's youngest billionaire as the co-founder of the app Snap. Luckily, he was very interested in affecting change in the place he had heard so much about for the past several years: Stockton.

Shortly after my election night party, which he attended, I went down to have dinner with him in Los Angeles to catch up on life. We talked about our upcoming weddings and some of the pressures we felt as young executives in very visible roles. We marveled at how far we had come in just seven short years and laughed at what our friends in South

Africa must be thinking when they read about us in the news. Deep into the conversation, Evan asked what I was working on and I shared with him breathlessly the outlines of the Stockton Scholars Program: an investment that would ensure for a decade every kid from the largest school district in the city would be guaranteed a scholarship to a trade school, a community college, or a four-year university.

He responded with a twenty-million-dollar pledge, which launched the program. Lange and I created a foundation to administer the scholarships, provide the support services, and bring other philanthropic investments into the city. We named it the Reinvent Stockton Foundation, and Lange was its first executive director. Under the program, students who graduate high school are guaranteed one thousand dollars a year for four years if they go to a four-year school. For 90 percent of our kids, based on their income, that makes Cal State tuition-free. They receive five hundred dollars a year for two years to go to community college. Or five hundred dollars a year for two years to go to a trade school. So, no matter which path they choose, there's money to support it. The message is simple: you have to do something after school, and we will support you financially to do it. Over time, we hope, we'll create that culture of expectation.

We leveraged the Stockton Scholars program to get education policy changes as well. The district has hired more counselors to keep up with the number of kids who want to go to college. High school graduation requirements have been aligned to meet college entrance requirements, which will take our A-G (California college entrance requirements completion rate) from just 35 percent to closer to 90 percent in the next five years.

Like SEED, the Stockton Scholars program is personal to me, a kid who made good thanks to life-changing opportunities. I look forward to watching our city and state transform as thousands of Michael Tubbses graduate from Stockton schools every year.

When I think about what committed me to public service for life, my first answer is clear: the murder of my cousin Donnell. My mayoral campaign promised to lower the city's gun violence and homicide rates, and I was prepared to do that by any means necessary.

In working with Chief Jones and others as a councilmember, I had already seen gun violence deterrence programs at work. As we implemented our Operation Ceasefire, engaging with those most likely to contribute to gun violence in our community (with lots of technical assistance from the California Partnership for Safe Communities), and established the Office of Violence Prevention, we went from seventy-one to thirty-two homicides in 2012–2013. This success was short-lived, however. During each of my last three years on the council we had forty-nine homicides every year.

Given the longstanding nature of the problem, the scale and scope of it, I knew we needed more than one intervention to ensure a lasting reduction in violence and to establish a new baseline. New analysis revealed that less than 1 percent of our 315,000 population committed 80 percent of our gun crimes—250 individuals. As small a share of the population as this was, it was more than we were equipped for. Our Office of Violence Prevention and our Peacekeepers had the capacity to work with eighty people, which left 170 high-risk men in need of services.

I decided to bring the Advance Peace program to Stockton to complement our Ceasefire work. Created by Devonne Boggan in Richmond, California, Advance Peace shared with Ceasefire the root conviction that the men involved in gun violence aren't necessarily the problem, and that they have to become a part of the solution. Both strategies understand that those involved in gun violence are likely to be victims as well as perpetrators. They have high rates of trauma, they have been shot at, they've known people who have been shot. That doesn't excuse their behavior, but it helps explain it. As a community, we have to see these folks as worthy of care, compassion, dignity, and healing. Through Advance Peace, we gave these men attention, social services, educational opportunities, tattoo removals, and, in some cases, even cash.

That last offering, part of a fellowship within the program, has become a lightning rod for criticism. It reduced the strategy to "cash for criminals," when it can be more aptly described as care and concern for community. As a program working with high-risk individuals, Advance Peace doesn't share their client list, but it has been inspiring to see how they've employed men like our former gang member Peacekeepers— once part of the problem, now part of the solution. Some of these men have told me they know my father.

Early signs of our strategy are promising, with a 40 percent reduction in homicides in 2018 and 2019 over the five-year average, and a 30 percent reduction in violent crime.

Governing is a fight. Despite success and national acclaim for many of the programs I instituted, and other indicators that the city was improving (we went from post-bankruptcy to ranking as the second most fiscally healthy city in California, and from being named "most miserable city" to one of the top 100 places to live by *Forbes* magazine and *U.S. News & World Report*, respectively), I encountered a lot of hate too.

This was nurtured and fanned by a tabloid site created the month that I was sworn into office, which manufactured crisis after crisis and published fabricated stories that played on anti-Black bias and caricatured me as a drug addict, a criminal, and someone who was fleecing the taxpayers of their hard-earned money. It popped up at the same time our one local newspaper was scaling down significantly, creating a news desert and information vacuum: the perfect grounds for disinformation to flourish. This "news" site was founded by members of Mayor Silva's camp, including Motecuzoma Patrick Sanchez, a disgruntled political loser with an envy-induced vendetta against me. Rumor had it that their funding came from Mayor Silva's political consultant and from leaders of the far right in this country.

Throughout my tenure as mayor I sought to minimize their reach and credibility, calling them our local OAN and Breitbart News networks. I was sure the community would see how obvious it was that my wedding was not paid for with city funds, that my staff didn't make one hundred fifty thousand dollars each, that nearly a thousand students every year were in fact receiving scholarships, and that I wasn't constantly under FBI investigation. Sadly, I was blind to what the site knew well: that civic illiteracy, racism, and a distrust of government can make even the most blatant lies true enough to cloud perceptions of progress.

The clearest example of the impact of this disinformation and the latent racism I encountered during my tenure was during a discussion I brought to the council about ending the city's golf subsidy. Every year, even during bankruptcy, the golf subsidy had increased, even as we were unable to open libraries that had been closed during bankruptcy or fund other essential services. A decade prior, the council tried to halt the subsidy but was unable to do so, as they were fearful of angering constituents. I had a bias for action, however.

The city operated two public courses despite the dozen or so private golf clubs—including those both cheaper to use and open to the public!—in a ten-mile radius. One public option, the Van Buskirk Municipal Golf Course, had been neglected for generations and was located in my old council district, right next to the gym where I had launched my political career. The course was situated on more than 100 acres of underutilized land, in a community that was 90 percent minority, and right next to an affordable housing project. The kids in the neighborhood were more interested in soccer, basketball, football— really, any other sport—and I marveled at the fact that even though I grew up close to the course, I never realized it was there. I just thought it was a massive, unkept yellow lawn.

The second golf course, Swenson Golf Course, was located in a more affluent part of town, surrounded by streets named after Confederate generals: Calhoun Way after Sen. John C. Calhoun, a leading champion of slavery; Gordon Court after a leader in Georgia's postwar KKK; Stonewall Court after Stonewall Jackson. Houses around the golf course are valued at at least half a million dollars, yet many of these were part of the county but not incorporated in the city, meaning their taxes did not go to the city coffers to pay for the upkeep. It was the taxes of less well-off residents, who didn't even use the golf course, that created the subsidy that in turn juiced the home equity of those who lived by the golf course.

As the subsidy kept increasing while play at these courses decreased, I grew frustrated. When city staff informed me that we didn't have money to create an Affordable Housing Trust, I saw an opportunity to kill two birds with one stone: a new reason to end a parasitic subsidy, and a creative solution to a pressing city need.

I didn't recognize at the time that golf was a third-rail issue, but I did know that it served as a proxy for age, class, race, gender, and power. Still, when the future of the public courses was put to the city council, I was not prepared for the backlash.

As soon as word of the scheduled discussion got out, disinformation began to work, and racism reared its ugly head. The newly formed disinformation "news" site and Councilmember Christina Fugazi (Mayor Silva's vice-mayor) proclaimed that I had struck a deal with Bay Area developers to develop the golf course for affordable housing. The community needed to rally together to "Save Swenson and Stop Mayor Tubbs," they proclaimed. The day of the council discussion, upwards of 100 residents came to the council meeting to berate me for threatening their "heritage and way of life," mortgaging their children's future, and being bought by the highest bidder.

Interestingly, only four or five of the dozens of cards came from the community near Van Buskirk golf course.

I looked at the city manager and my council incredulous—how the hell did one budget allocation become the biggest political crisis in the city, more controversial than bankruptcy and homicides? I was just trying to solve a problem and continue a discussion that had begun when I was a high school senior.

Unannounced, I attended a meeting held at the golf course of more than four hundred residents, many of whom were older and white. To my chagrin, they had signs made in big black letters that said, SAVE SWENSON, STOP MAYOR TUBBS and were passing them out to everybody in attendance. I worked my way to the front of the crowd and made my case while clearing up the disinformation. I didn't have the power to act unilaterally, this was not a new discussion, we had to end the golf subsidy, and the city needed funding for affordable housing projects.

Walking back to my car, my staff flanked me tightly, nervous about the possibility of mob violence—people had been that worked up. "Who is this boy to think he could do this?" "He must be stopped at all costs!" were refrains I heard that day. Almost at the car, a twentysomething white man approached me with a STOP MAYOR TUBBS sign in his hand and jeered, "You are helping your hood, I'm going to protect mine."

The entire city is my hood, I thought. And we aren't going to turn the golf course into a battleground for some new kind of gang warfare.

Midway through another town hall meeting, during a presentation from the Swenson district's councilmember, an elderly white woman stood up to point at me and exclaim: "WE DON'T TRUST YOU!" Thunderous applause rolled from the audience. I looked around, confused, as I hadn't spoken—the councilmember, the deputy city manager, and the private golf course operators were on the night's docket; I was there to listen. But the damage was done. The young Black mayor didn't like white people and was taking away their golf course to build affordable housing in a Machiavellian plot to make their community "ghetto" like my own, as many of the constituent emails I received claimed.

My team and supporters were stressed, worried that this episode would derail other progressive work we were doing, but I loved the prospect of solving a problem other councils and mayors hadn't dared to approach. It wasn't easy, but I brought together supporters of the "Save Swenson, Stop Mayor Tubbs" group to create a solution-oriented working group. I allowed them to interview city staff and look at the books, and they all came to the same conclusion: the only way to save Swenson was, in fact, to end the city subsidy. Over the course of a year, we came to the conclusion that Swenson would remain a golf course, but as a private operation, from which the city would be paid 10 percent of its profits.

Not surprisingly, there was very little effort to "Save Van Buskirk." One of the scenarios posited by the Save Swenson group was that the city should cease paying for anything at Van Buskirk and should use those funds to invest in Swenson.

I did not appreciate this episode's full undertones until we had accomplished the mission. This was about North versus South, it was about old versus new, it was about change, and it was about whether a young Black man should be trusted with power. It left me a bit wiser as to how it wasn't just the message that impacted how people responded to me, it was also the messenger. Disinformation campaigns preyed on people's biases and fears to slow down progress and undermine my ability to govern. To this day, some residents believe that I had made a deal to sell the golf course and was going to use a vendetta I had against white people to build affordable housing there. (As if white folks don't need housing they can afford too!)

The political is personal. Those closest to the pain should be closest to the power. The deeper the roots, the deeper the commitment to making structural change should be. I was committed to using my experiences and the experiences of all of my constituents, in particular the most marginalized, to create an administration grounded in the simple notion of the dignity of all people. I drew on the triumphs and challenges in the lives of my mom, my aunt, Nana, my father, my brother and cousins, my classmates, and my students, to think about what policies could have changed their environments. I drew on my own improbable story for the faith to push for more and dream of better, and to remind myself that structure doesn't have the last word. That there is still agency. Still life. That roses shouldn't have to grow from concrete, but they can and will, while we dig up all the concrete and plant rosebushes. My survivor's guilt is part of my fuel, and memories of my childhood both haunt and inspire me to be bold and dream big, to push against a failing status quo, to be audacious enough to assert that we all deserve better and are entitled to baseline dignity and real opportunity.

On October 19, 1972, Michael Anthony Tubbs, my father, was born.

On August 2, 1990, Michael Derrick Tubbs was born, greeted with the nervous anticipation of three young Black women who committed to giving him a chance against the steep odds that had led his father to be, at that moment and for the next three decades, incarcerated.

On October 19, 2019, at 9:04 A.M., Anna gave birth to our son, Michael Malakai Tubbs, Jr.

We were at St. Joseph's Hospital in Stockton, California, overwhelmed with joy. Born on the same day as his grandfather, Michael Malakai's birth represents a new beginning and a new opportunity to illustrate to the world what Michael Tubbs can do when given a chance.

Vice President (then Senator) Kamala Harris called to wish

my son well, and our local newspaper ran a front-page story on the birth of this little Black boy who happened to be the son of the mayor and the First Partner. State elected officials sent proclamations announcing his birth, and our friends and relatives spoke confidently on the impact that he was going to have in the world. I am so thankful for these affirmations for my son, particularly in a time when many children, especially Black children in the United States, are greeted with messages that suggest the opposite, messages that they weren't planned, that they'll be lucky to make it past twenty-one, that they are a drain to the state, that they are defined by the mistakes of the adults in their lives, that they have no path for upward mobility, that they are disposable. The birth of my son has only furthered my resolve to create a world that values all people. I want every child to be greeted just like the third Michael Tubbs.

Although my son is born into a level of privilege I could not have dreamed about as a child, he is still a Black person in America, and I am under no illusions about the obstacles he will have to face. Anna and I want to impart to him many of the lessons my three mothers taught me: that he matters, that it is important how you treat people, and that he has the duty to change the things in the world that he finds to be unjust or unacceptable. We also want to add the nugget that he shouldn't apologize for his privilege, but that he should think about how to give purpose to it.

For Michael Malakai, I want a world in which his ethnicity doesn't destine him for negative encounters with police, lower expectations of his capacities and intelligence, biased chances for jobs and loans, and an earlier death. I want a world that treats everyone as neighbors, a world that guarantees not equal outcomes, but fair ones, a world that ensures that our structures and institutions are reflective of our best values. I want his society to recognize the inherent and universal dignity of all people. I want a world that is not perfect, but just.

As mayor, I also think a lot about the Stockton that I want my son to grow up in. I want him to be proud, to be able to say: "I'm from Stockton! It's a great place." I want him to learn as much from the city as I've learned—that Chipotle is good, but taco trucks are better, that scraped knees from playing rec league basketball build character, that the most amazing people are the ones you see every day doing the normal, heroic work of coaching, mentoring, and parenting. I want him to learn how to dance to "Suavemente," the customs of the Sikh temple, the ways in which Stockton natives like Larry Itliong and Dolores Huerta changed this country, and how to know how to be tenacious but loving at the same time. I want him to know that joy and pain can coexist, that family matters and community are important. I hope he learns that, however far you grow, it's that much sweeter when you have deep roots.

The summer of 2011 was the fiftieth anniversary of the 1961 Freedom Rides, whose participants protested the ongoing Jim Crow segregation of interstate buses in the South in the years after the Supreme Court had deemed segregation unconstitutional. I was fortunate to spend ten days reenacting the Freedom Rides with some of the original Freedom Riders. We stopped at the same places they had stopped in 1961, and I took the opportunity to ask them about the choices they made then, and what they had done since. I was struck by how they were simultaneously ordinary people and extraordinary heroes. Many of them had gone on to be accountants and bus drivers and teachers.

Bob Singleton is a former professor of economics. Before the Freedom Rides, he had served in the army, and then, while he was studying economics at UCLA, he was inspired by the speakers who came to the campus, including Malcolm X, James Baldwin, and Langston Hughes, each of whom helped him realize the injustices in America. He became president of the NAACP at UCLA and led sit-ins and advocated for sharecroppers to get the vote before organizing and participating in the Freedom Rides.

As the bus trundled toward Anniston, Alabama, Bob posed a question to me.

"Michael," he said.

I said, "Yes, sir."

"I was arrested on August 4, 1961. Now why is that day important?"

It came out of nowhere, his question, but I knew I should convey my gratitude for what he'd done.

"Well, you were arrested. If you weren't arrested, we wouldn't be on this bus. We wouldn't have the rights we enjoy today."

He rolled his eyes and said, "No, son." He continued: "On that day, Barack Obama was born."

Bob Singleton said he had no idea at the time, as a twenty-year-old in 1961, that the choice he was making would enable someone fifty years later to have a chance to be president, someone who was born on that day with no opportunity.

Then Bob looked at me and asked: "What are you prepared to do today, so that fifty years from now a child is born with more opportunity?"

Today, as I write this, I ask myself: What am I prepared to do so that, fifty years from now, our sons and daughters are born into a world worthy of them?

What are you prepared to do?

Let's do it together.

EPILOGUE: GOD'S PLAN

The Get Out the Vote weekend was upon us, and I had not decided whether I wanted to host a reelection party. The year 2020 was grueling, as I learned how to be a father while leading a city during a pandemic. For months, I had spent almost every night on Zoom calls with other California mayors, working to provide for our people amidst the total absence of federal leadership.

I worked fourteen- to sixteen-hour remote days with my team, studying the emerging science of how COVID-19 spread while also trying to meet the basic needs of our many constituents who were laid off and/or homebound during the shutdown.

We created the Stockton Strong Coalition, which delivered food to our elderly neighbors and those living in food deserts. I raised millions of dollars to support small businesses and nonprofits while working with the governor to create a free drive-through testing facility in Stockton. Most of these efforts were a battle with councilmembers who downplayed the seriousness of the crisis and its impact on our most vulnerable populations, with constituents who advocated a misguided understanding of "herd immunity," and from the mostly white and conservative San Joaquin County Board of Supervisors, the governing body responsible for leading the cities in their jurisdiction during the crisis. The board's leadership parroted Fox News talking points about needing to open up our economy and COVID-19 being no worse than the flu.

In this climate, I could feel the political ground shifting under my feet. The consensus I had spent so much time forging, with my four-Republican, two-Democrat council, weakened. Every COVID-19-related proposal I put forward was met with resistance the likes of which I hadn't seen since the Swenson golf course fight. I tried to bring our city laws in line with state laws regarding eviction moratoriums and was voted down four to three despite homelessness being the council's stated top priority.

In June, because the county wouldn't, I put on the agenda a commonsense mask ordinance. Given our case numbers at the time, some of the worst in the state, I wrongly assumed that the proposal would be met with a reluctant thank-you. Instead, it was met with downright hostility. The head of emergency services for the county told me to "stay in my lane" (I could hear the unspoken "boy" at the end of the declaration) and ultimately the proposal was voted down by the city council, six to one. I couldn't get a single colleague to risk the backlash of doing what was right for public health and the most vulnerable members of our community.

I was incensed after that vote. I told my staff: there's something weird afoot here. People aren't responding to my leadership.

That instinct was right.

I was often too busy with reality to worry about politics. Stockton was not immune to the outrage and pain that 2020's police brutality brought into mainstream American consciousness. After the murder of George Floyd, I worked with Chief Jones and our new city manager, Harry Black, to create a new slate of police reforms, including a Community Review Board and more community outreach. I met with protestors and, working collaboratively, was able to ensure that no arrests, no tear gas, no curfew, and no National Guard interfered with their movements. I also created Mayors for a Guaranteed Income, a nationwide network of mayors committed to seeing a federal guaranteed income policy as a response to what COVID-19 and the civil unrest of our cities have shown us: that the status quo is untenable.

I decided the day before the 2020 election to host a watch party: a small, intimate, COVID-19-responsible gathering on the rooftop of a restaurant in downtown Stockton. Given the leadership my administration had exhibited during the crisis, the thirteen-million-dollar budget surplus we were projecting for the end of this year—during a recession and a pandemic—and the gains we had made on homelessness and other civic issues, I was confident that I would be the first mayor of Stockton to be reelected since 2000.

Anna and I brought Malakai to vote with us on Election Day at city hall, and the energy felt victorious. After we voted, the poll worker shared how proud she was and mused that we might be related. A passing driver screamed, "We love you, Tubbs!"

A heckler followed with "We are going to get you out," but we shrugged. After eight years in local government, Anna and I were accustomed to potshots.

The mood at the election party was solemn, with everyone spaced out and wearing masks as the early national returns showed Trump winning in several swing states. "This feels so different than last time," Anna said.

"Yeah, I know. Like a funeral. Trump can't win again though, and we can't lose. I blame COVID for the mood."

Anna smiled through her mask and we went around the tables, thanking the fifty or so attendees for their support. My mom had elected to stay home and watch Malakai, saying she was more tired than excited about the elections this year. Nana stayed home as well, a collective decision of the family because of her susceptibility to COVID-19, but also because she had been recently diagnosed with pancreatic cancer. Tasha and Papa were there representing the family, as confident as ever that this election party would end up like the ones we'd held over the previous eight years.

At 9:00 P.M., first results were slated to be released. At 9:03 P.M., no word from my campaign team about how much of a lead were we starting with. Anxious and annoyed, I asked them for an update. I was losing the early vote by five hundred votes. I had never seen myself behind in an election, so I asked, "How the hell did this happen? What's going on?" I was met with an IDK.

Five hundred votes wasn't that bad, so I told the gathered press that I would do interviews at 10:00 P.M., once more votes had been counted. At 10:05 P.M., though, I was down by one thousand votes. Anna rushed to my side, reminding me to be strong for those gathered. It appeared that Biden was losing too, based on the votes that had been counted. Tasha told me how proud she was and gave me a big hug.

I walked up to the mic with no notes and no idea what I was going to say. I spoke directly from the heart.

"The last four years haven't been a fight about me. They have been a fight about you and what type of community your children deserve to live in, what type of educational opportunities they should have, whether you deserve an income floor, whether people deserve second chances and we deserve safety and the opportunity to heal from trauma."

I was still confident we would win but, whatever happened, I said, "We have to remind ourselves that progress comes at a price. We are in for a fight: a fight to live our lives with dignity, a fight to ensure that this city belongs to everybody."

Everyone departed, hopeful that the next day would bring good news, but it didn't. Lange and I were both losing by more than the night before, as were many of our elected allies. For two weeks we monitored the results, hoping for a flip when the mail-in votes were tallied, but the margin just kept increasing. Every night at 9:00 P.M., when the new vote tallies came in, my phone was flooded with messages of dismay. Every day thereafter, I was a bit angry, confused, and embarrassed. Until finally, I conceded. I realized the cavalry wasn't coming, that this door was shut, and that clearly God had another plan in mind. I was the youngest mayor, and now I was the youngest ex-mayor.

I found solace in the Scriptures and gospel music, in playing with my son, in decompressing with my wife, and in taking stock of all that had been accomplished in eight years. I became proud of the fact that, even in elected office, with pushback and a platform, I was clear about my sense of purpose. Yes, I lost, but not because nothing had changed, nor because things were worse, nor because I had changed. I lost because I had shown what was possible, and because progress comes at a price. I was proud of having made people so uncomfortable that they launched a four-year disinformation campaign against me, saddling me with every anti-Black trope: that I was lazy, that I was stealing money from the city, that I was a crook, and I was a criminal. I was and am none of those things. I was effective. I was bold. I was in love with possibility—and I remain those things.

The last disbursement of the SEED program was in February 2021. I had decided to extend the program when it was slated to end in July 2020 because of the economic impact of COVID and was able to partner with philanthropist Carol Tolan to do so. After two years and the completed analysis of survey and spending data from our research team in March 2021, I announced the findings of SEED. Our recipients had experienced reduced income volatility, or the month-to-month income changes households face, and had actually worked more than they had outside the program, thanks to finding full-time employment at a higher rate. Recipients were also mentally healthier, reporting less depression and anxiety.

Based on these results, more than fifty mayors have signed on to support guaranteed income, either through piloting similar programs in their own cities, or advocating for it as a federal policy, or as part of Mayors for a Guaranteed Income. The federal government is catching on, too. Stimulus checks have been the most popular part of federal COVID-19 recovery bills, and President Biden has guaranteed income for families with children through a monthly child tax credit. This has provided millions of families what I did for 125 families in Stockton: the dignity of being able to breathe and to have the agency to make the right decision for themselves and their families.

Complicated feelings about home are a given because growth and pain are often two sides of the same coin. I am thankful for everything my city has taught me, and for the opportunity to lead at such a pivotal time in our city's and country's history. I won't say I don't harbor disappointment at the slander—and, frankly, abuse—I endured as a public official, but from those trials I learn the work yet to do. There is much to celebrate in Stockton, much to look forward to, and, still, much to change.

At the onset of my thirties I am in a similar position as I was a decade earlier at the onset of my twenties: dealing with the pain of a loss and figuring out my path forward. My twenties started with the murder of Donnell, which pushed me to look to return home to run for city council. My thirties started with a year that included a global pandemic and a national reckoning on race, coupled with a surprising, very public reelection loss. I am confident, however, "that he who began a good work in you will carry it on to completion" (Philippians 1:6). In this moment, I am doing my best to learn all I can from this new valley experience, arming myself with the wisdom, resilience, and strength needed to continue to fight and to climb and conquer new mountains.

"What's it like being a Black mayor?" This question has caused me more difficulty than any other over the years. And it was never more persistent than during 2020, first because of the havoc wrought by COVID-19 and the acute devastation faced by the Black community, and then because of the righteous protests that sprung up after the executions of Breonna Taylor and George Floyd.

The urgency and the complexity of the crises caused me to depend even more heavily on my tendency to do rather than feel, and Anna saw that it was taking its toll. I was working hard, and things were moving, but Anna thought it would be wise for me to take a beat. To stop. To feel. With her wisdom, she pulled me aside after another marathon day upon hearing my frustration in sharing with constituents what we were doing to be responsive to the moment. She grabbed my hands to get my attention, looked me in my eyes, and said, "Babe, people are also interested in how you personally feel in this moment. They want to know that you are human, and that you are hurting, too."

Anna's redirection was a necessary one, putting into focus for me one of the functions of white supremacy: to dehumanize, either causing us to see others as nonhuman, or to force ourselves to be superhuman in compensation. To not feel, to not grieve, to not hurt—just to do. Anna's insight caused me to well up with tears as, for one of the first times in my life, I gave myself permission to be vulnerable. My emotions bubbled up: I felt hurt, I felt angry, I felt sad, I felt that more needed to be done, I felt doubt about whether the work that I had dedicated my life to was worth it, I felt scared for Michael Malakai. As a Black human in the United States of America in 2020, I felt a shared experience that James Baldwin diagnosed when he said, "To be a Negro in this country and to be relatively conscious is to be in a state of rage almost, almost all of the time."

The feeling I had in 2020 because of COVID-19 and the extrajudicial murders of Black people, and that I still have today, is the same rage I felt the entire four years with Donald Trump in the White House, which was the same rage I felt when I was repeatedly kicked out of class, or told that I was going to Stanford just because I was Black, which was the same rage I had at my father's incarceration, which was the same rage I had while watching my mom, aunt, and nana put in superhuman effort to raise me and my siblings, which was the same rage I felt when Donnell was murdered, which was the same rage that brought me to run for city council and for mayor.

Yes, this rage is not new. It's a companion that I've learned to channel into inspiration, into energy to ensure the setup is as upset as I am. As *we* are. Upset. This rage is rooted in faith, the substance of the things hoped for and the evidence of things not seen, an active faith that is alive with works, with communal efforts to ensure our better angels are reflected in the type of society we build. This rage is rooted in love, a deep, abiding love in the possibilities of the future, in the best of all of us, a love that is not anemic, but ferocious in demanding more, in wanting better for all of us.

Rage. Faith. Love. The three stones I will wield, that we will wield, as righteous weapons to ensure liberty and justice once and for all.

ACKNOWLEDGMENTS

Life is a team sport, and my life even more so. Accordingly, this memoir owes a lot to countless people named and unnamed. Like any good church boy, I have to start with giving all honor to God and my Lord and Savior Jesus Christ. Through much prayer and much meditation on Scripture I've learned and grown and have so much more to do.

I also have to give a huge thanks to my three mothers: my mom, Racole Dixon; my auntie, Tasha Dixon; and my nana, Barbara Nicholson. A cord of three strands cannot be broken. You all are the sheroes of this story and deserve volumes written about who you all are and what you all have accomplished. Your sacrifices and your love are the real ink in these pages.

My partner, Anna Malaika Nti-Asare-Tubbs, from the first time I met you, you've intrigued, inspired, and challenged me and I am so thankful to learn from you every day. Your love and your partnership are the wind beneath my wings. Michael Malakai and Nehemiah, your births were the impetus behind me finishing and going deep to write a story that you all can refer to in the years to come as you seek to write your own. Shaleeka, Scharlyce, and Dre—a whole 'nother volume could be written about the unit we formed growing up and all of our shenanigans. Thank you for being the best siblings one can ask for and for your constant support and love. My church families and pastors like Alfred and Shields and parishioners like Sister Kim, thank you for helping me find and let this little light of mine shine.

Book writing is incredibly hard and so many people pushed and supported me through this process. My agent, Betsy Lerner, and dear friend Jodi Solomon, thank you for believing that this story was one worthy to be told. My amazing editor, Meghan Houser, you are a magician with the pen—your intellect and empathy made the arduous rewrites manageable. Ariane Conrad, thank you for your insight, background research on Stockton before I arrived on the scene, and for helping in capturing stories of loved ones that I may have lost. Chris Hughes and Steve Phillips, thank you for your support and for believing that this book would indeed be finished one day! Alex, Tiq, Cameron—thank you for helping to read early drafts, for checking in, and for pushing me when needed. Oprah, Alice Walker, and Valerie Jarrett—thank you for being such catalytic and willing vessels for me to find my purpose during pivotal inflection points. I hope you all are proud of the ways you have contributed to what I've accomplished and who I am becoming

Stockton. My home. My origin. Thank you for the opportunity of a lifetime. For the lessons taught and the victories won and everything in between—I appreciate it all. I was blessed to have an amazing ecosystem of leaders, staff, and supporters to work with—thanks to each and every one of

ACKNOWLEDGMENTS

you. To my staff in the mayor's office: Jasmine, Cameron B. (the Swiss Army Knife!), Alvin, Daniel, Max, Sukhi, Ann, Mehraan, and Rhonnalyn. Hope you all have caught your breath and taken a moment to reflect on the crazy productive four years we had. Florence Low, administrative support extraordinaire—thank you for all the support you provided me as a councilmember and as mayor. Lange. Enough said. The Reinvent Stockton Universe, the Foundation, the Reinvent South Stockton Coalition, councilmembers like Moses Zapien, Dyane Burgos, Jesus Andrade, the best vice-mayor ever Elbert Holman, Kathy Miller, Chief Eric Jones, and the other amazing public servants I have been able to work with—look at what we were able to accomplish. Supporters like the nonprofit all-stars, Michael, Dea and Natalia, Michael and Gia D., Jane, Christy Wise, and Carol Tolan, I learned so much from all of you and appreciate the ways we were able to work together.

And thank you for reading.

ABOUT THE AUTHOR

MICHAEL TUBBS served as the seventy-ninth mayor of Stockton, California, his hometown. He was the city's first Black mayor and the youngest-ever mayor of a major American city. He is the founder of Mayors for a Guaranteed Income and Ending Poverty in California and a special adviser to California governor Gavin Newsom on Economic Mobility. Tubbs has been a fellow at the Harvard Institute of Politics, the MIT Media Lab, and the Stanford Design School. He has also served as a Stockton city council member and a high school educator. He lives with his partner, Anna Malaika Tubbs, and their children.